D0520696

CUISINART®
FOOD PROCESSOR
COOKING

CUISINART®

# FOOD PROCESSOR COOKING

**Revised and Expanded Edition**

CARMEL BERMAN REINGOLD

A DELTA BOOK

A DELTA BOOK

Published by
Dell Publishing Co., Inc.
1 Dag Hammarskjold Plaza
New York, New York 10017

CUISINART is the registered trademark of
Cuisinarts, Inc. of Greenwich, Connecticut.

Copyright © 1976, 1981 by Carmel Berman Reingold

All rights reserved. No part of this book may be reproduced
or transmitted in any form or by any means, electronic or
mechanical, including photocopying, recording or by
any information storage and retrieval system,
without the written permission of the
Publisher, except where permitted by law.

Delta® TM 755118,
Dell Publishing Co., Inc.
Printed in the United States of America
9 8 7 6 5 4 3 2

# Acknowledgments

My thanks to my readers: all those people who like to cook and use food processors, and who have taken the time to write and tell me how much they enjoyed the previous edition of this book. Many offered suggestions as to what to include in this updated and revised edition, and the section on Chinese cooking is dedicated to all those who asked for Chinese recipes adapted to food processors. The section on baby food is offered with thanks to Wendy Fingerhut, whose idea it was, and a special thanks to Gail Piazza, a fine home economist, who helped me test the recipes contained herein.

# Contents

# THE WONDERFUL WORLD OF THE FOOD PROCESSOR

When food processors were first introduced to the American market a few years ago, they truly created a revolution in the kitchen. They were fast to catch on with the public, and more and more companies are now manufacturing them. The recipes in this book can be used in your favorite processor—be it old or new, large or small.

People who love to cook have discovered that they can embark on more ambitious gourmet meals, their tasks made easier by food processors. Others, who are not that interested in involved recipes, also enjoy using the food processor: cooking chores have been simplified, and far less time has to be spent in the kitchen.

At first it seemed as though food processors might only be used by a few enthusiasts, but as more people became familiar with these wonderful machines, it became clear that processors were for everyone who did any cooking at all. Why stand by a cutting board slicing cabbage for cole slaw, when a food processor could shred pounds of cabbage in a minute? People who loved Steak Tartare realized that they could now easily grind the fresh meat necessary for this dish. Piecrusts? A food processor kneaded perfect piecrust dough in seconds.

Today many people feel that there are additional advantages to food processors. They're a great joy to people who prefer eating at home but who don't have unlimited time to spend in the kitchen. And with restaurant prices on the rise, more people are becoming involved in home cooking. Food processors are also a favorite with people who reject food that's loaded with salt, sugar, additives, and preservatives. They know that when they prepare baby food, mayonnaise, peanut butter, or jam in the food processor, they control the ingredients.

What are some of the tasks that a food processor can perform? In addition to the ones already mentioned, processors can

- grind meats for pâtés, sausages, meat loaves
- chop vegetables for stews, soups, casseroles
- shred potatoes for pancakes
- puree vegetables
- puree fruits for jam
- slice zucchini, potatoes, tomatoes
- grate fresh horseradish
- grate bread for crumbs
- chop and slice for Chinese or Japanese cooking
- knead dough for pasta
- knead dough for breads and pies
- prepare cookie and pastry dough
- prepare pancake and crêpe batter.

# The Changing Food Processor

Have food processors changed during the last few years? Yes, and they have gotten better. When the first food processors came on the scene, it was so wonderful to have an extra pair of hands in the kitchen that it seemed impossible that these machines could be improved upon. But today's processors do even more than their predecessors of only a few years ago. This does not mean that you should discard the processor that you may now have in your kitchen; follow the instructions below for adapting your machine to the newer techniques.

One big change in the world of food processors is that most of the current models are based on the same design: A base houses the motor, and a work bowl sits on the base. The discs or blades—and most machines come with a metal chopping blade, a slicing blade or disc, and a shredding or grating blade or disc—fit into the bowl.

# New Techniques in Processing

**Pulse-On-Off Lever**

Many manufacturers, such as Cuisinarts, Inc., Farberware, Moulinex, Waring, General Electric, and others, now offer food processors with a Pulse-On-Off Lever. This lever, which enables you to perform a quick, short burst of processing, makes it a lot easier to control the degree of processing. You can turn the machine on and off more quickly, stopping to scrape down the sides of the bowl for a more uniform texture.

*If Your Machine Doesn't Have a Pulse-On-Off Lever*

Follow the directions in the recipes and turn the machine to Off when it says Pulse-On-Off. Scrape down the sides of the bowl and turn to On once again. This takes very little extra effort when you consider how quickly all processors work.

**Speed Control**

At this time, three machines—Farberware, Hamilton Beach, and Sunbeam processors—have levers that control speed. Such levers are very handy when preparing a dish in which some ingre-

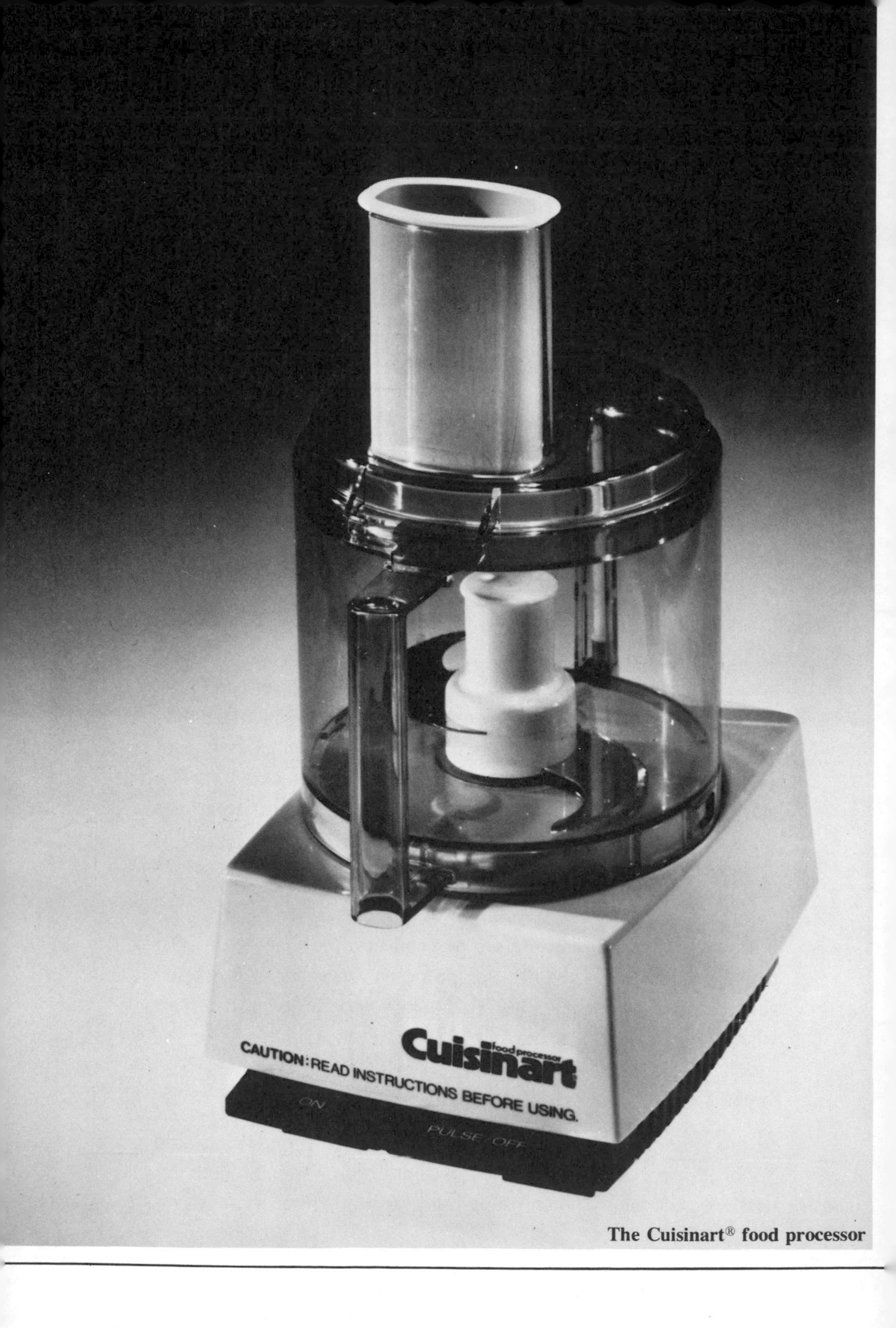


**The Cuisinart® food processor**

**The new Cuisinart® machines have expanded feed tubes as standard equipment.**

**The new Cuisinart® dough kneading blade makes it possible to mix and knead over two pounds of yeast dough at a time.**

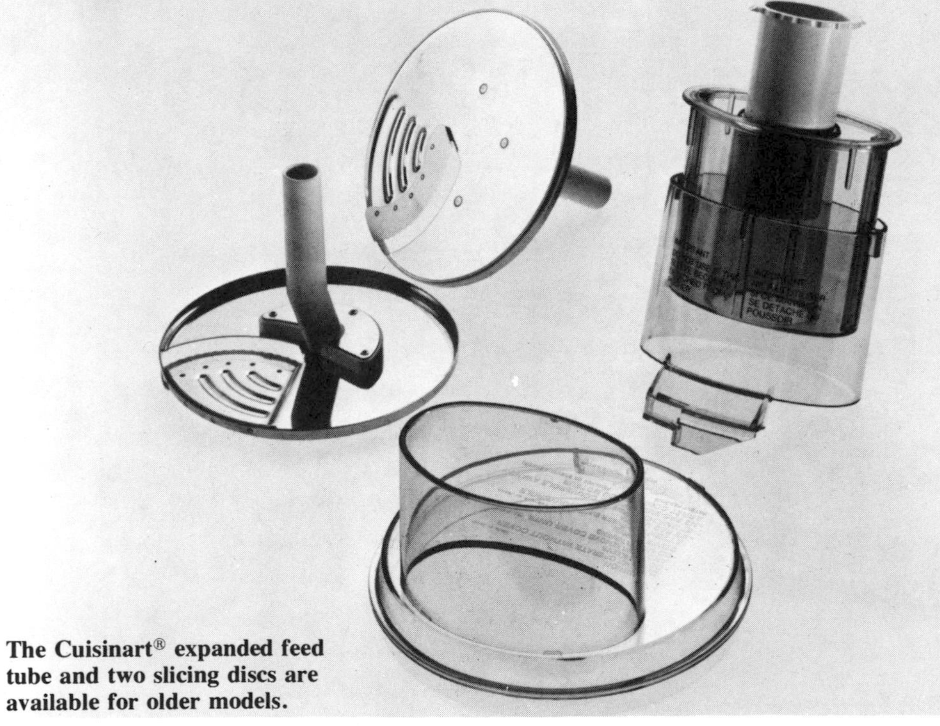

**The Cuisinart® expanded feed tube and two slicing discs are available for older models.**

**The Moulinex® La Machine III food processor plus mixer. This model features a second bowl for convenience.**

**The General Electric® food processor**

**The Farberware® food processor**

dients have to be pureed while others call for chopping. For example, if you're making a tuna or crabmeat salad, puree the tuna or crabmeat with the mayonnaise at a high speed and then add the celery and process at a lower speed so that the celery is chopped and blended into the fish without being liquified.

*If Your Machine Doesn't Have a Speed Control Lever*

You can still control the speed of your machine by using the Pulse-On-Off Lever, or by turning the machine on and off, or by processing the ingredients separately, and then combining them for one final, quick blending.

## Expanded Feed Tube

The newer Cuisinart food processor models have expanded feed tubes as standard equipment. However, expanded feed tube kits with additional slicing discs are available for older models. You'll find an expanded feed tube wonderfully useful when you want to slice whole, large potatoes, onions, oranges, and tomatoes. (Yes, you can slice tomatoes without squashing them.) The additional slicing discs enable you to make long French fries and to julienne potatoes, zucchini, and pineapple.

*If Your Machine Doesn't Have an Expanded Feed Tube*

Other machines, such as the Farberware unit, also slice tomatoes—albeit smaller ones—beautifully. Use smaller vegetables if you wish to slice them whole, or cut them in half to facilitate slicing. If you have a vegetable or fruit—a lemon, for example—that is too big to go through the feed tube, try loading the tube from the bottom and then placing the cover on top.

## Larger Processor Bowls with Greater Capacity

Some processors, such as the Cuisinart machine, come with larger work bowls, which will enable you to process large quantities at one time. You can grind two pounds of meat for a meat

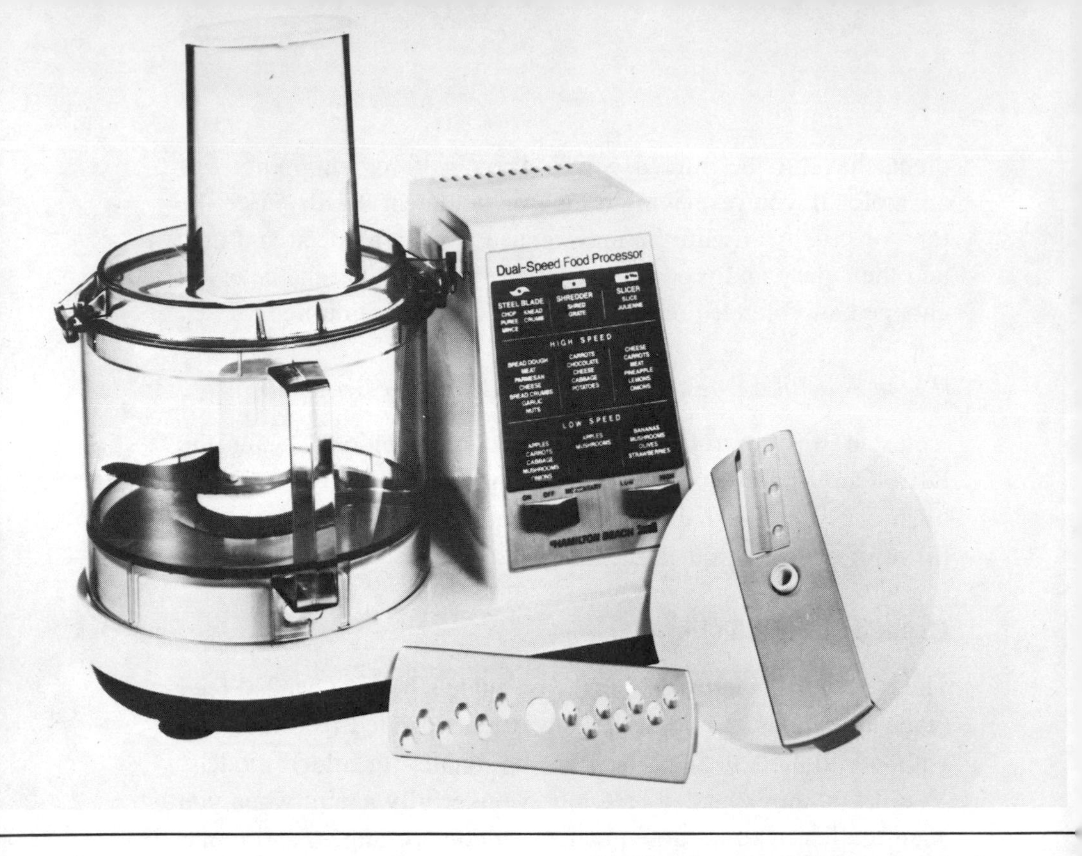


**The Hamilton Beach® two-speed food processo**

loaf, and you can make breads and cakes with the heavier dough that previously had to be kneaded in machines equipped with a dough hook.

*If Your Machine Doesn't Have a Larger Processor Bowl*

All food processors work so quickly that it doesn't take too much more time—maybe an extra minute or two—to process food in two or more steps. Chop or puree half the ingredients, remove from the processor to another bowl, and then process the remainder.

The special section on bread and pastry recipes for large-capacity processors explains how you can adapt the recipes in that section to smaller capacity processors. If you wish, the recipes can also be prepared in machines equipped with dough hooks.

**Accessory for Whipping Cream and Beating Egg Whites**

At this time, Moulinex offers a new accessory that truly whips cream, and turns egg whites into the peaks of a proper meringue.

*If Your Machine Doesn't Have an Accessory for Whipping Cream and Beating Egg Whites*

You can prepare a thickened heavy cream in most processors by using the metal blade and chilling the blade, the bowl, and the cream in the freezer for about 15 minutes. Cream will be thick enough for many recipes, but it will not have the volume of air beaten into it of true whipped cream.

You cannot beat egg whites in a processor that does not have the proper accessory. Use a whisk, or a small hand or electric beater instead.

# When Using Any Food Processor:

- If you've just bought a food processor, read all the information provided by the manufacturer and follow all directions and precautions.

- Be careful when placing blades or discs in, or removing them from, the processor bowl. Blades and discs are very sharp and should be carefully stored out of the reach of children.

- Don't lift the cover of a food processor until the machine has come to a complete halt. An impetuous turn of the cover while the blades are still whirling can result in a counter covered with tomato sauce, or the like.

- Use the food pusher and never place your fingers in the feed tube.

**The Sunbeam® Food Preparation Center**

- When mashing or pureeing potatoes, turn machine on and off, using pulse lever if your machine has one and scraping down sides of the bowl frequently. Do not overprocess, or potatoes will have an unpleasant, pastelike texture.

- Do not overprocess cookie, bread, cake, and pastry dough, or dough will be too heavy.

- When chopping garlic, slices of ginger, or other small, hard foods, drop into machine through feed tube while the machine is on.

- Regulate the size of chopped foods by turning machine on and off, using pulse lever if your machine has one, and scraping down the sides of the bowl.

# APPETIZERS

Who doesn't love the little nibbles and snacks that precede a meal? For many people these amount to their favorite course, and for the person who is doing the entertaining, they offer the best opportunity to present a variety of unusual dishes.

Consider doing a dinner composed entirely of appetizers! In a way, this goes along with the *nouvelle cuisine*—the new cuisine developed in France: course after course is presented, but each course is no more than a few rich and savory mouthfuls. Appetizers and hors d'oeuvres also make entertaining easier because guests help themselves, and food can often be picked up with the fingers.

Some appetizers—the ones that concentrate on vegetables—are also beloved by dieters. They're delicious, low in calories, and so satisfying that there's no danger of arriving at the dinner table in a state of semistarvation and thus consuming too much food.

Don't limit appetizer offerings to company meals. One or two hors d'oeuvres presented before a family dinner, and offered with spiced tomato juice, wine, or a drink, make any meal something special and any evening just a little more festive.

# Céleri Rave Rémoulade

**1 pound celery root, peeled and cut in half**
**1 teaspoon salt**
**3 teaspoons lemon juice**
**6 tablespoons mayonnaise**
**Salt and freshly ground black pepper to taste**

Place slicing disc in food processor. Slice celery root. Remove slicing disc and place shredder in food processor. Shred celery root slices.

Remove shredded celery root and sprinkle with salt and lemon juice. Toss, and allow celery root to marinate for 30 minutes. Rinse celery root, drain, and dry on paper towels.

Combine celery root, mayonnaise, and seasoning. Mix thoroughly and refrigerate for at least 2 hours before serving. This dish is especially good if prepared with homemade mayonnaise (see Mayonnaise recipes on pages 60–61).

**Serves:** 6 to 8

# Eggplant Caviar

*It may be Eggplant Caviar in English, but to the Rumanians, who insist they invented this dish, it's called* Putla Jel. *By either name, it's an unusual appetizer that goes especially well with Mideastern pita bread and your favorite cocktail.*

**1 large eggplant**
**1 medium onion, peeled and cut in half**
**1 small green pepper, seeded and sliced**
**Juice of ½ lemon**
**½ cup olive oil (or more, to taste)**
**Salt and freshly ground black pepper to taste**
**¼ teaspoon sharp red pepper flakes (optional)**

Place eggplant in broiler and broil until skin is charred and eggplant is soft to the touch. Turn eggplant every 10 minutes or so. Eggplant will be cooked in 20 to 30 minutes, depending on size of vegetable and your broiler.

Place metal blade in food processor. Chop onion and green pepper in processor. Pieces should be in small chunks; be careful not to overprocess. Remove onion and green pepper, and reserve.

When eggplant is cooked, remove from broiler and allow to cool. Peel, and cut eggplant into large pieces. Using metal blade again, puree eggplant, pulsing on and off, and gradually add lemon, olive oil, and seasonings to processor.

Remove pureed eggplant from processor and stir in chopped onion and green pepper. Chill before serving.

**Serves:** 4 to 6

# Eggplant Puree

*This delightful appetizer is served at the Intercontinental Hotel in Old Jerusalem.*

**1 large eggplant**
**1 clove garlic, peeled**
**⅓ cup tahini (sesame seed paste)**
**Juice of 1 lemon**
**⅓ teaspoon ground cumin**
**Salt to taste**
**Freshly ground black pepper to taste**
**1 tablespoon olive oil**

Broil eggplant, turning from side to side, until skin is charred and eggplant is soft to the touch. Depending on the size of your eggplant and broiler, this should take from 20 to 30 minutes.

Remove eggplant from the broiler. Allow to cool. Peel, and cut eggplant into chunks. Place metal blade in food processor. Add eggplant to processor and pulse on and off for 1 minute. Scrape down sides of the bowl and add all other ingredients to processor.

Puree eggplant, combining thoroughly with all other ingredients, pulsing on and off, for another minute or two. Ingredients should be completely blended. Correct seasoning and serve as a dip with large, flat, Mideastern pita bread, or with sesame seed crackers.

**Serves:** 4 to 6

# Hummus Bi Tahini

*"What is it? How do you make it?" Be prepared for questions when you serve this interesting mixture of chick peas and sesame seed paste. The ingredients may not seem so fascinating by themselves, but in combination they create a culinary delight. The origin of this dish is Mideastern; and if you want to sound truly knowledgeable,* hummus *is the word for chick peas, and* tahini *signifies the rich sesame seed paste.*

**1 cup cooked chick peas**
**2 tablespoons olive oil**
**Juice of 1 lemon**
**1 clove garlic, peeled**
**½ cup tahini (sesame seed paste)**
**¼ to ½ cup water**
**Salt and freshly ground white pepper to taste**
**Paprika**

Place metal blade in food processor. Add chick peas, olive oil, and lemon juice to processor and puree, pulsing on and off. With machine on, drop garlic through feed tube into processor and pulse on and off for another 30 seconds.

Add tahini to processor. Scrape down sides of bowl and pulse on and off. Add water gradually. Mixture should be a fairly thick, creamy mass. Season with salt and white pepper to taste.

Spoon hummus into a glass bowl. Garnish with paprika and serve with pita bread or crackers.

**Serves:** 4 to 6

# Shrimp Toast

**6 canned water chestnuts**
**⅓-inch piece fresh ginger**
**½ pound shrimp, shelled and deveined**
**1 scallion, cut into 3 pieces**
**1 egg yolk**
**1½ teaspoons cornstarch**
**1 tablespoon dry sherry**
**Salt to taste**
**Freshly ground black pepper to taste**
**2 egg whites**
**2 cups vegetable oil**
**3 slices slightly stale white bread, crusts trimmed, cut into quarters**

Place metal blade in food processor. Add water chestnuts and ginger to processor and chop fine. Add shrimp, scallion, and egg yolk, and pulse on and off until ingredients are blended. Add cornstarch and sherry, scrape down bowl, and continue processing until mixture is a paste. Add seasonings and process until blended. Remove shrimp mixture to a large bowl and reserve. Remove metal blade and wash and dry processor bowl thoroughly.

Place plastic blade in processor. Add egg whites to processor and beat until thick. Using a spatula or large spoon (do not use processor), fold egg whites into shrimp mixture.

Heat vegetable oil in a wok or a large skillet. Spread bread quarters with shrimp mixture and slip bread into hot oil, shrimp side down. Fry until brown, and turn and brown on other side. Remove from pan, drain, and serve at once.

**Serves:** 4 to 5

*Mr. T. T. Wang owns and is the chef at Shun Lee Palace, one of the best Chinese restaurants in New York. Mr. Wang, who was introduced to us by one of his captains, Eddie Liu, has generously shared two of his very special appetizer recipes.*

# T. T. Wang's Chinese Shrimp Strawberries

**1 cup hulled sesame seeds**
**1 tablespoon red food coloring (optional)**
**½ pound shrimp, shelled and deveined**
**2 water chestnuts**
**1 egg white**
**½ teaspoon salt**
**1 grind of white pepper**
**1 tablespoon dry sherry**
**1 tablespoon cornstarch**
**1 teaspoon sesame oil**
**12 two-inch-long strips of green pepper, sliced thin**
**4 cups salad oil**

Mix sesame seeds with food coloring and spread seeds on an ovenproof dish. Place dish in a 200-degree oven for 5 to 7 minutes. Stir seeds once or twice and remove dish from oven when seeds are dry.

Place metal blade in food processor. Add shrimp, water chestnuts, egg white, salt, pepper, sherry, cornstarch, and sesame oil to processor. Pulse on and off and scrape mixture down from sides of bowl until mixture is a thick paste.

Spoon mixture into a bowl and refrigerate for ½ hour.

*To Form Strawberries:*
Take 1 tablespoon of shrimp mixture, form into a ball shape, and roll in colored sesame seeds until shrimp ball is well coated with

seeds. Form each shrimp ball into a strawberry shape and decorate with a green pepper strip for the stem. Refrigerate Shrimp Strawberries for an hour or so, until they are firm.

Heat salad oil in a deep fryer, wok, or large skillet until oil is sizzling hot. Fry strawberries approximately 3 to 5 minutes on each side, until they are crisp. Drain and serve at once. You'll have about 12 strawberries.

**Serves:** 3 to 4

# T. T. Wang's Green Pepper Puffs

**3 small green peppers, cored and seeded**
**2 water chestnuts**
**¼ pound lean pork, trimmed and cut into cubes**
**1 scallion, cut into 3 pieces**
**2 egg whites**
**1 teaspoon dry sherry**
**½ teaspoon salt**
**1 grind white pepper**
**½ teaspoon sesame oil**
**½ tablespoon cornstarch**
**½ cup all-purpose flour**
**¼ cup water**
**1 teaspoon salad oil**
**1 teaspoon baking powder**
**4 cups salad oil**

Cut peppers into wide strips. Three peppers should yield 12 pieces. Discard seeds and membrane. Place metal blade in food processor. Add water chestnuts, pork cubes, scallion pieces, and one egg white to processor. Process until pureed. Add sherry, salt, pepper, sesame oil, and cornstarch to bowl and pulse on and off until mixture is a smooth paste. Scrape down sides of bowl from time to time so that all ingredients are thoroughly blended. Remove mixture from processor and spread on green pepper strips, smoothing with the back of a spoon or fingers.

Wash bowl and dry. Place metal blade in processor once again. Add second egg white, flour, water, 1 teaspoon of salad oil, and baking powder to processor. Blend thoroughly. Using a pastry brush or spoon, coat each slice of stuffed pepper with batter.

Heat salad oil in a deep fryer, wok, or large skillet until oil is sizzling. Reduce heat and cook puffs in oil, about 5 minutes on each side, until they are golden brown. Don't reduce the cooking time, or pork may not be cooked sufficiently.

Drain, and serve at once.

**Serves:** 3 to 4

# Gail's Deviled Eggs

**1 dozen hard-cooked eggs, peeled and halved lengthwise**
**½ cup homemade Mayonnaise (see pages 60–61)**
**½ small onion, peeled**
**1 teaspoon lemon juice**
**1 teaspoon Dijon mustard**
**¼ teaspoon salt**
**¼ teaspoon freshly ground white pepper**
**2 sprigs parsley**
**Sweet paprika**

Place metal blade in food processor. Remove egg yolks from whites. Reserve whites. Place all ingredients except egg whites and paprika in processor and blend until smooth, about 20 seconds. With a spoon or pastry tube, fill egg-white halves with yolk mixture. Sprinkle eggs with paprika.

**Serves:** 8 to 10

# Ham Devilish Eggs

**8 hard-cooked eggs, peeled and halved lengthwise**
**½ cup mayonnaise**
**2 to 3 small sweet pickles, cut in half**
**1 teaspoon Dijon mustard**
**Salt and freshly ground white pepper to taste**
**1 or 2 slices of boiled ham, cut into 4 or 5 pieces**
**¼ teaspoon mild paprika**
**3 slices sweet pickle, cut into slivers**

Place metal blade in food processor. Remove yolks from whites. Reserve whites. Place all ingredients except egg whites and sweet pickle in processor and blend until mixture is thoroughly smooth. With a spoon or pastry tube, fill egg-white halves with yolk mixture. Garnish with pickle slivers.

**Serves:** 6 to 8

# Lenke's Hungarian Egg Salad

*American egg salad always seemed bland to my mother, who makes her egg salad with onions, rendered chicken fat, and plenty of black pepper. This piquant version takes egg salad out of the ordinary category.*

**8 hard-cooked eggs, peeled and halved**
**1 large onion, peeled and cut into quarters**
**½ cup rendered chicken fat**
**Salt and freshly ground black pepper to taste**

Place metal blade in food processor. Add eggs to processor. Pulse on and off for 30 seconds. Add remainder of ingredients to processor and pulse on and off, scraping down sides of bowl from time to time. Egg mixture should contain pieces of chopped onion. If you want a smoother egg salad, continue processing. You may add more chicken fat if you wish.

This egg salad should be fairly spicy. Serve a large dollop of egg salad on lettuce leaves or use as a spread for cocktail-size sandwiches.

**Serves:** 4 to 5

# Hungarian Lecso and Smoked Sausage

*Hungary, a small and not terribly rich country, is the source of many fine recipes that make a little meat go a long way. But no Hungarian worthy of the name would touch a money-saving recipe that was flat or uninteresting. Here's a spicy appetizer that's inexpensive but rich in flavor.*

**½ cup olive oil**
**2 medium onions, peeled**
**2 large green bell peppers, seeded and cut into 2 pieces**
**1 pound very ripe red tomatoes**
**2 teaspoons sugar**
**¼ teaspoon salt**
**½ tablespoon sweet paprika**
**½ teaspoon hot paprika, or to taste**
**½ pound Hungarian cooked and smoked Kolbasz sausage, or your favorite smoked sausage**

Place metal blade in food processor. Heat olive oil in a large skillet and, while oil is heating, place onions and green pepper in food processor and chop coarsely. Pieces should be fairly large. Remove onion and green pepper from processor and add to skillet. Cook over low heat for 10 to 15 minutes, or until onion is translucent and pepper limp.

Place tomatoes in processor and puree coarsely. Add tomatoes and sugar, salt, and paprikas to skillet and cook, stirring, for an additional 10 minutes.

Place slicing disc in food processor and slice sausage. Add sausage slices to skillet and cook, stirring, until all ingredients are thoroughly hot. Correct seasoning. Serve with hand-cut, large slices of caraway-seeded rye bread and dry red wine or beer.

**Serves:** 4 to 6

# Taramasalata

*This fish roe appetizer has long been a favorite of guests at Greek and Mideastern restaurants. Tarama is the salted and dried pressed roe of the gray mullet and is found canned in many small Greek food shops and gourmet stores. If you can't find tarama, you can use smoked cod's roe, available in stores that sell smoked fish. If you use smoked cod's roe, remember to remove the outer membrane before proceeding with the recipe.*

**3 slices thick-cut white bread**
**1 cup milk**
**3 ounces tarama**
**1 clove garlic, peeled**
**Salt and white pepper to taste**
**1 slice of onion**
**Juice of 1 lemon**
**6 tablespoons olive oil**

Cut crusts from bread and soak slices in milk. Place metal blade in food processor and add tarama to processor. Chop thoroughly. Squeeze milk from bread and add bread, garlic, salt, white pepper, and onion to processor. Pulse on and off, scraping mixture from sides of bowl. Turn processor on and gradually add lemon juice and olive oil to mixture in processor. Continue processing, by pulsing on and off, until mixture is thoroughly blended and is a light, creamy, pink paste. Serve with Mideastern pita bread and tiny, Greek black olives.

**Serves:** 4

# Avocado Tuna Spread

**2 medium, ripe avocados, peeled and cut into large pieces**
**1 seven-ounce can tuna, drained**
**½ cup mayonnaise, or more, to taste**
**Dash of Tabasco**
**Salt to taste**
**Freshly ground black pepper to taste**

Place metal blade in food processor and add all ingredients to processor. Pulse on and off, scraping down sides of bowl from time to time, until all ingredients are a smooth blend. Correct seasoning and serve with buttered rounds of sourdough bread or rolls.

**Serves:** 6 to 8

# Frilly Dip

**½ head iceberg lettuce**
**4 tablespoons olive oil**
**2 tablespoons wine vinegar**
**2 scallions**
**¼ teaspoon salt**
**Freshly ground black pepper to taste**
**¼ teaspoon thyme**
**¼ teaspoon sage**
**1 eight-ounce package cream cheese, cut into 4 pieces**

Place metal blade in food processor. Add ¼ head of lettuce and all other ingredients except cream cheese to processor. Pulse on and off, scraping down sides of bowl from time to time, until lettuce is coarsely chopped and combined with other ingredients. Add cream cheese and remainder of lettuce and process until mixture is blended. Correct seasoning. Serve with crackers or toasted pumpernickel fingers.

**Serves:** 4 to 6

# Dutch Cheese Balls

**1 three-inch round Edam cheese, with red wax coat**
**¼ pound sweet butter, cut into 6 or 7 pieces**
**½ teaspoon sharp mustard**
**1 tablespoon brandy**
**Dash of Tabasco**
**¼ teaspoon mild paprika**

Place metal blade in food processor. Slice off top of cheese and, with a knife or a melon ball cutter, scoop out as much cheese as possible, leaving outside shell intact. Place cheese and all other ingredients in processor and pulse on and off until thoroughly blended. Scrape down sides of bowl from time to time. Pile mixture back into hollowed cheese shell and garnish with a few more shakes of paprika.

**Serves:** 6 to 10

# Camembert Cashew Appetizer

*Traveling around the country and demonstrating the wonderful uses of the food processor, I discovered that this appetizer was a favorite. No matter how much was prepared, it was quickly devoured. You'll get the same reaction when you serve it at your house.*

**12 to 15 cashew nuts**
**¼ pound sweet butter**
**¼ pound Camembert cheese, room temperature**
**¼ cup sweet white wine**

Toast cashews in a 300-degree oven until nuts are lightly browned, approximately 3 to 5 minutes. Be careful not to burn them. Place metal blade in food processor. Add nuts to processor and grind until fine. Cut butter into 6 or 7 pieces and place in processor. Gently remove rind from Camembert, cut cheese in 6 or 7 pieces, and add to processor. Add wine. Pulse on and off, scraping mixture down from sides of bowl, until all ingredients are thoroughly blended. Do not overprocess or butter will melt. Spoon cheese mixture into a bowl and chill. Serve with crackers and celery and carrot sticks.

**Serves:** 4 to 6

# Biscuits of Brie

**4 ounces ripe Bric cheese**
**2 ounces sweet butter, room temperature**
**1 egg**
**¼ teaspoon salt**
**2 or 3 grinds of white pepper**
**Pinch of cayenne pepper**
**1 cup all-purpose flour**

Place metal blade in food processor. Gently remove crust from Brie. Cut cheese into chunks, and place in processor. Cut butter into two pieces and add to processor. Add egg and seasoning. Pulse on and off until all ingredients are blended. With processor on, gradually add flour to cheese mixture. Once all flour is in processor bowl, pulse machine on and off, scraping dough down from sides of bowl, until dough is thoroughly blended. If dough seems too soft, add another tablespoon of flour. Remove dough from processor, wrap in wax paper, and chill until firm.

Roll biscuit dough out until it is about ¼ inch thick, cut into 1-inch rounds, and place on cookie sheet. Heat oven to 350 degrees and bake for 15 to 20 minutes or until biscuits are lightly browned.

**Serves:** 4 to 6

# Pineapple Walnut Spread

**1 eight-ounce package cream cheese, cut into 6 pieces**
**½ cup shelled walnuts**
**3 slices canned pineapple**
**1 tablespoon pineapple syrup**
**⅛ teaspoon cinnamon**

Place metal blade in food processor. Add all ingredients to processor. Chop and blend until smooth. Serve with date-nut bread or thin toast fingers.

**Serves:** 4 to 6

# Irene's Caraway Cheese Spread

**1 three-ounce package cream cheese, cut into 3 pieces**
**¼ pound sweet butter, cut into 5 to 6 pieces**
**1 small onion, peeled and cut into quarters**
**½ teaspoon mild paprika**
**¼ teaspoon caraway seeds**

Place metal blade in food processor. Add all ingredients to processor. Blend thoroughly. Pile into a dish or bowl and garnish with a sprinkling of paprika on top. Serve with crackers and slices of cucumber.

**Serves:** 6 to 8

# Spring Salad Dip

**1 stalk celery, cut into 3 pieces**
**1 carrot, cleaned, scraped, and cut into 3 pieces**
**¼ green pepper**
**2 radishes**
**3 slices sweet cucumber pickle**
**3 sprigs parsley**
**1 teaspoon dried chives**
**1 pimiento**
**½ teaspoon salt**
**¼ teaspoon freshly ground black pepper**
**1 eight-ounce package cream cheese, cut into 3 pieces**

Place metal blade in food processor. Add all ingredients, except cream cheese, to processor. Pulse on and off until all vegetables are chopped. Add cream cheese and continue processing, scraping mixture down from sides of bowl, until mixture is thoroughly blended and smooth. Use as a dip with fresh raw vegetables or with crackers.

**Serves:** 4 to 5

# Flavored Butters

*In France, butter comes in many more flavors than just salt or sweet. These* beurres composés *are available in endless variety and are created by combining butter with herbs, spices, raw vegetables, and fish. These seasoned butters can be used to flavor other dishes, or they can be used as dips and as spreads. Keep a small pot of* beurre composé *in your refrigerator to create an instant hors d'oeuvre for unexpected company or to use as a topping for vegetables.*

# Anchovy Butter

**1 two-ounce can anchovies, drained**
**1 scallion, cut into 2 or 3 pieces**
**¼ pound sweet butter, cut into 4 to 6 pieces**

Place metal blade in food processor. Add anchovies and scallion to processor and chop. Scrape down sides of bowl and chop once again. Add butter to processor and pulse on and off, until all ingredients are thoroughly blended.

**Yield:** Approximately ½ cup

# Herb Butter

**¼ cup mixed fresh dill, parsley, and chives**
**¼ pound sweet butter, cut into 4 to 6 pieces**

Place metal blade in food processor. Add herbs to processor and chop. Scrape down sides of bowl and chop once again. Add butter to processor and pulse on and off until mixture is thoroughly smooth and blended.

**Yield:** Approximately ½ cup

# Lemon Parsley Butter

**¼ cup fresh Italian parsley**
**1 tablespoon lemon juice**
**¼ pound sweet butter, cut into 4 to 6 pieces**
**1 tablespoon heavy sweet cream**
**3 grinds white pepper**

Place metal blade in food processor. Add parsley to processor and chop. Add all other ingredients to processor and pulse on and off, scraping down sides of bowl, until mixture is thoroughly smooth and blended.

**Yield:** Approximately ½ cup

# Nutty Butter

**1 cup mixed nuts**
**¼ pound sweet butter, cut into 4 to 6 pieces**
**Salt to taste**

Place metal blade in food processor. Add nuts to processor and chop. Scrape down sides of bowl and chop again. Add butter and salt and pulse on and off, scraping down sides of bowl until mixture is smoothly blended.

**Yield:** Approximately 1 cup

# Tuna Butter

**¼ pound sweet butter, slightly softened and cut into 4 to 6 pieces**
**½ cup drained tuna fish**
**1 hard-boiled egg, peeled and halved**
**½ small onion, peeled**
**1 teaspoon lemon juice**
**Salt and freshly ground black pepper to taste**

Place metal blade in food processor. Add all ingredients to processor and pulse on and off, scraping mixture down from sides of bowl until ingredients are thoroughly blended.

**Yield:** Approximately 1 cup

# Dips for Crudités

*Sticks and rounds of raw vegetables—crunchy, colorful, delicious—are made even more delicious when dipped into the spicy and creamy sauces that are so quickly prepared in the food processor.*

*Buy vegetables in season for the most delectable results. Tiny red radishes or peeled slices of black radish, carrots and celery cut into sticks, cauliflower separated into flowerets, and zucchini and cucumber sliced into rounds by the food processor, all create an interesting offering of raw vegetables (call them* crudités *if you wish to be French and fashionable). Present them with a variety of dips, happily acknowledging that, yes, the dips are rich, but the vegetables are so low in calories that all diet-conscious guests can eat and be happy.*

# Dill Sour Cream Dip

**½ cup sour cream**
**½ cup mayonnaise**
**¼ teaspoon white pepper**
**8 sprigs fresh dill**

Place metal blade in food processor. Add all ingredients to processor and pulse on and off, scraping down sides of bowl, until all ingredients are thoroughly blended.

**Yield:** Approximately 1 cup

# Garlicky Dip

**1 cup sour cream**
**1 three-ounce package cream cheese, cut in half**
**1 clove garlic, peeled**
**¼ teaspoon salt**
**4 grinds black pepper**

Place metal blade in food processor. Add sour cream and cream cheese to processor. Pulse on and off until blended. With machine on, add garlic and blend another 30 seconds. Scrape down sides of bowl, add seasoning, and process until mixture is smooth and thoroughly blended.

**Yield:** Approximately 1½ cups

# East Indian Dip

**1 cup yogurt**
**½ teaspoon curry powder**
**¼ teaspoon ground cumin**

Place plastic blade in food processor. Add all ingredients and pulse on and off, scraping down sides of bowl, until all ingredients are thoroughly blended.

**Yield:** Approximately 1 cup

# Double-Crème Dip

**1 eight-ounce package cream cheese, cut into 3 pieces**
**1 cup heavy cream**
**1 clove garlic, peeled**
**1 scallion, cut into 2 pieces**
**Salt and freshly ground black pepper to taste**

Place metal blade in food processor. Add cream cheese and heavy cream to processor. Pulse on and off until cream cheese and cream are blended, scraping down sides of bowl. With machine on, add garlic and scallion and pulse on and off until ingredients are blended. Add seasoning and process until seasoning is blended into other ingredients.

**Yield:** Approximately 2 cups

# Spiced Cabbage in Pastry

*Want to amaze your guests with something really different? Offer them slices of flaky pastry filled with sweet and spicy cabbage. It's a mid-European favorite, not as yet well-known among American gourmets. It looks like an elaborate appetizer when presented, but thanks to the use of packaged pastry leaves and a processed filling, it's not all that difficult to prepare.*

**FILLING**

**2 pounds white cabbage**
**Salt**
**¼ pound butter**
**4 tablespoons sugar (or more to taste)**
**Freshly ground black pepper to taste**
**½ cup dark raisins**

**PASTRY**

**2 sheets packaged strudel or phyllo leaves**
**4 tablespoons melted butter**
**4 tablespoons bread crumbs**

*To Make Filling:*

Place shredding disc in food processor. Shred cabbage. You might have to do this in more than one step, depending on the size of your processor bowl. Place all shredded cabbage in a bowl and sprinkle lightly with salt. Allow salted cabbage to stand for 1 hour. By that time salt will have drawn water out of the cabbage. Squeeze handfuls of cabbage, pressing out the water. Rinse cabbage thoroughly, or it will be too salty, and squeeze out water once again.

Heat half the butter in a large skillet. Add half the cabbage and half the sugar. Sauté the cabbage, stirring from time to time, until cabbage is a golden brown. Repeat with remaining cabbage and sugar. Season cabbage generously with pepper and stir in raisins. Reserve cabbage mixture.

*To Make Pastry:*

Prepare strudel or phyllo leaves according to package directions. Spread 2 tablespoons of melted butter over 1 sheet of pastry and sprinkle with 2 tablespoons bread crumbs. Place second sheet of pastry over first and repeat.

Spread cabbage mixture on long side of pastry, and roll jelly-roll fashion. Place cabbage-filled pastry on a lightly buttered cookie sheet and bake in a preheated 375-degree oven for 30 minutes. This pastry should be served warm and can be prepared in advance and reheated. Cut into 2-inch slices before serving. Perfect with before-dinner drinks.

**Serves:** 6 to 8

# Vegetable Pizza

**½ cup warm water**
**1 quarter-ounce package active dry yeast**
**¼ teaspoon sugar**
**1¾ cups all-purpose flour**
**½ teaspoon salt**
**¼ teaspoon freshly ground black pepper**
**3 small firm ripe tomatoes**
**2 small zucchini**
**¼ pound fresh mushrooms**
**1 medium onion, peeled**
**½ pound mozzarella or Monterey Jack cheese**
**½ teaspoon basil, crushed**
**½ teaspoon oregano**
**2 tablespoons Parmesan cheese, grated**

Place plastic or metal blade in food processor. Add warm water to bowl and sprinkle sugar and yeast over water. Allow to stand 5 minutes. Add 1½ cups flour, salt, and pepper to bowl. Pulse on and off for 10 seconds or until all ingredients are thoroughly blended. Add remaining flour, pulsing on and off until dough begins to form a ball. Dough will be soft.

Using a spatula, remove dough to a lightly floured board. Knead in just enough flour so that dough is smooth and elastic and bounces back when touched. Place dough in a floured bowl. Cover and allow to rise in a warm, draft-free place for 2 to 3 hours, or until dough has doubled in bulk.

While dough is rising, peel tomatoes. The simplest way to do this is to place tomatoes in boiling water for 30 seconds. Remove tomatoes with a slotted spoon and allow to cool. Skin will peel off easily at this point. Remove cores. Place slicing disc in food processor. Individually slice tomatoes, zucchini, mushrooms, onions, and cheese. Remove each item after slicing.

Stretch dough to fit a 10-inch pizza pan. Arrange vegetable slices on dough, cover with cheese, and sprinkle seasonings and Parmesan cheese on top. Bake pizza in a preheated 450-degree oven for 20 minutes or until crust is brown, vegetables are hot, and cheese is melted.

**Serves:** 6 to 8

# Onion Tart

**PASTRY**

**1⅓ cups all-purpose flour**
**¼ pound butter**
**¼ teaspoon salt**
**2 to 3 tablespoons ice water**

**FILLING**

**4 medium onions, peeled and thinly sliced**
**¼ pound butter**
**½ teaspoon salt**
**¼ teaspoon freshly ground white pepper**
**5 eggs, lightly beaten**
**1½ cups light cream**
**1 tablespoon Parmesan cheese, grated**
**1 tablespoon all-purpose flour**

*To Make Pastry:*

Place metal blade in food processor. Add flour, butter, and salt. Process until the mixture has the consistency of coarse meal. With the machine running, add water to the processor. Continue processing until mixture forms a ball. Refrigerate at least 30 minutes before using.

*To Make Filling:*

Place slicing disc in food processor. Slice onions. Sauté onions in butter, stirring, until onions are translucent. Combine onions with all other ingredients, mixing well.

Roll out dough on a lightly floured board and fit into a 9-inch pie plate. Pour filling into crust. Bake in preheated 350-degree oven for 30 to 40 minutes or until knife inserted 1 inch from center comes out dry.

**Serves:** 6 to 8

# Mediterranean Carrot Appetizer

*This is one of those simple— and simply delicious—appetizers that everyone loves. For best results buy young, thin carrots, not the thick, woody kind that are really meant for preparing beef stock.*

**6 carrots, cleaned and scraped**
**½ cup olive oil or more as needed**
**2 tablespoons wine vinegar**
**2 cloves garlic, peeled**
**8 sprigs parsley**
**Freshly ground black pepper to taste**

Place shredding disc in food processor. Shred carrots and remove to bowl. Combine oil and vinegar, mixing well, and pour over carrots, tossing, to coat carrots thoroughly. Place metal blade in food processor. With machine on, drop garlic into processor. Turn machine off and place parsley in processor. Chop, scraping down sides of bowl, for approximately 15 seconds. Add garlic and parsley to carrots, season with black pepper, and mix to combine thoroughly.

**Serves:** 6 to 8

# SOUPS

Soups, wonderful soups. Cold and creamy Vichyssoise in July, spicy Mexican Black Bean soup to add warmth to cold February. Soups can be presented as a first course, or they can be—with the addition of crusty bread and sweet butter—a meal in themselves.

Soups have been known to soothe, but scientists have only recently confirmed that some hot soups really do help the person suffering with a cold. How nice to know that there is some truth to what had been regarded as one of Great-Grandmother's tales.

Soups come in great variety, and thanks to the food processor, you can add to that variety, if you wish, by creating your own soup recipes. Just save those scraps of meat and bits of leftover vegetables in your refrigerator, puree, add broth and seasonings, and you will have created your own original soup.

Another advantage to soup cookery is that many of the recipes in this chapter can be prepared a day or more in advance. You can present a delicious and satisfying prelude to any meal without last-minute fuss and bother.

# Chicken Curry Soup

**1 carrot, cleaned, scraped, and cut into 3 or 4 pieces**
**2 onions, peeled and cut into quarters**
**2 stalks celery, each cut into 3 or 4 pieces**
**¼ pound butter**
**2 tablespoons all-purpose flour**
**1 tablespoon curry powder**
**1 large apple, peeled, cored, and quartered**
**2 cups cooked cubed chicken**
**8 cups chicken broth**
**Salt and freshly ground white pepper to taste**
**1 cup heavy sweet cream**

Place metal blade in food processor. Add carrot, onions, and celery to processor and chop. Heat butter in a large skillet and sauté vegetables until they're translucent. Add flour and curry powder and cook, stirring for 2 to 3 minutes. Place apple and chicken in food processor and, using metal blade, chop until fine. Add cooked vegetables to processor and gradually add 2 cups of chicken broth, blending thoroughly. When mixture is thoroughly blended, pour into a large saucepan and stir in remainder of chicken broth. Add seasonings. Bring to a simmer and cook for 10 minutes. Remove from heat and stir in cream. Serve hot.

**Serves:** 8 to 10

# Creamy Avocado Soup

**1 large ripe avocado, or 2 small ones**
**1 scallion, cut into 3 pieces**
**3 cups chicken broth**
**1 cup heavy sweet cream**
**Salt and freshly ground black pepper to taste**
**2 tablespoons freshly minced dill**

Place metal blade in food processor. Peel avocado, cut into chunks, and add to processor. Add scallion and puree thoroughly. Gradually add chicken broth and blend. Remove soup from processor and stir in cream. Season to taste. Chill. Garnish with minced dill when serving.

**Serves:** 6

# Danish Cucumber Soup

**5 medium cucumbers**
**½ medium onion, peeled and cut into 2 pieces**
**2 tablespoons butter**
**¼ cup all-purpose flour**
**2 quarts chicken broth**
**2 bay leaves**
**Salt and freshly ground white pepper to taste**
**1 cup light sweet cream**
**1 tablespoon lemon juice**
**8 sprigs fresh dill**

Peel cucumbers. Place slicing disc in food processor. Slice 1 cucumber and reserve. Place metal blade in food processor. Chop remaining cucumbers, remove from processor, and reserve. Chop onion in processor. Heat butter in a large saucepan and sauté chopped onion for 3 minutes. Blend in flour and cook an additional 3 minutes, stirring. Add chicken broth gradually, stirring. Add chopped cucumbers, bay leaves, salt, and pepper to soup. Cover, and simmer for 10 minutes. Remove bay leaves and puree soup in processor, using metal blade. Depending on the capacity of your processor bowl, you may have to do this in two or more steps. Return pureed soup to saucepan. Gradually stir in cream and lemon juice. Add cucumber slices and heat soup. Serve garnished with dill.

**Serves:** 8

# Chilled Pear Soup

**4 fresh pears, peeled, cored, and quartered**
**1 small apple, peeled, cored, and quartered**
**2 tablespoons lemon juice**
**1 potato, peeled and quartered**
**1 celery stalk, cut into 2 pieces**
**1 scallion, cut into 2 pieces**
**Salt to taste**
**¼ teaspoon curry powder**
**2 cups chicken broth**
**2 cups light sweet cream**
**Dash of cinnamon**

Place metal blade in food processor. Add pears, apple, lemon juice, potato, celery, and scallion to processor and chop. Remove mixture to a large saucepan and add salt, curry powder, and chicken broth. Bring to a simmer and cook uncovered for 10 minutes. Return soup to food processor and, using metal blade, blend until completely smooth. You may have to do this in two steps, depending on the capacity of your processor. Stir in cream and chill thoroughly. Serve garnished with a dash of cinnamon.

**Serves:** 6

# Fish Soup Bonne Auberge

*One summer in the south of France I had a dreadful cold, and reluctantly went off to the Bonne Auberge Restaurant, knowing that I wouldn't be able to eat a thing. The waitress looked at me sympathetically, and before I could explain that I wouldn't be eating dinner, she placed a large soup tureen in front of me, handed my husband the menu, and indicated that the soup was all for me. Only good manners made me taste it. It was hot and delicious, retaining the essence of the flavor of fish without being the least bit fishy. I ate every drop and felt completely revived.*

*The Mediterranean fish generally used in this recipe are not available in this country, but the soup can be made with other fish as long as they are fresh.*

**1 large onion, peeled and cut into quarters**
**4 cloves garlic, peeled and cut into halves**
**2 green peppers, seeded and each cut into 4 pieces**
**1 carrot, cleaned, scraped, and cut into 3 or 4 pieces**
**1 stalk celery, cut into 2 pieces**
**¼ cup olive oil**
**5 ripe tomatoes, peeled and cut in half**
**3 pounds fillets of assorted fish: cod, halibut, haddock, bass**
**½ teaspoon Herbes de Provence (or ¼ teaspoon thyme, 1 crushed bay leaf, and ¼ teaspoon fennel)**
**¼ teaspoon dried orange peel**
**1 cup dry white wine or dry vermouth**
**3 quarts water**
**Salt and freshly ground black pepper to taste**
**French bread rounds, toasted and rubbed with a cut garlic clove**

Place metal blade in food processor and chop onion, garlic, green peppers, carrot, and celery. Heat oil in large soup pot and add chopped vegetables. Cook over low heat until vegetables are tender, but do not let them brown. Chop tomatoes in food processor and add to pot. Cook, stirring constantly, for another 5 to 10 minutes.

Cut the fish fillets into cubes and add to vegetable mixture. Continue cooking for an additional 5 minutes and keep stirring. Stir in herbs and orange peel and add wine, water, salt, and pepper. Cover, bring to a simmer, and cook for 30 to 40 minutes.

Using metal blade, puree soup thoroughly in processor. You may have to do this in two or more steps. Return to soup pot and heat through. Correct seasoning and serve with a toasted French bread round in each bowl.

**Serves:** 8 to 10

# Chinese Good Fortune Fish Soup

**¾ pound fillet of sea bass or striped bass**
**2 egg whites**
**⅓ cup water**
**1 teaspoon salt**
**½ teaspoon sugar**
**1 tablespoon cornstarch**
**1 tablespoon peanut oil**
**5 cups chicken broth**
**2 scallions, chopped**
**¼ cup canned bean sprouts**
**6 water chestnuts, sliced**

Place metal blade in food processor. Make sure fish fillet is completely free of bones. Cut the fillet into chunks and put in processor. Add egg whites, water, salt, sugar, cornstarch, and oil and process until mixture is thoroughly blended into a paste.

Fill a large pot with two quarts of water. Form paste into 1-inch fish balls and drop into water. Bring water to a simmer and then remove fish balls to a large strainer or colander. Rinse fish balls with cold water.

Pour chicken broth into a large saucepan and add drained fish balls. Slowly bring broth to a simmer and simmer for 8 to 10 minutes. Add scallions, bean sprouts, and water chestnuts to broth. Correct seasoning and serve.

**Serves:** 6

# Vichyssoise

**2 leeks, white ends only, cut into pieces**
**1 medium onion, peeled and cut into quarters**
**3 tablespoons butter**
**4 medium potatoes, peeled**
**4 cups chicken broth**
**2 cups light sweet cream**
**Salt and freshly ground white pepper to taste**
**3 teaspoons chopped chives or scallion tops**

Place metal blade in food processor. Chop leeks and onion in processor. Heat butter in a large saucepan and sauté onion and leeks over low heat until vegetables are translucent. Place slicing disc in food processor. Slice potatoes and add to sautéed vegetables. Add chicken broth, cover, and cook until potatoes are tender. Allow soup to cool for 30 minutes. Place metal blade in food processor and puree soup, pulsing on and off. Do not overprocess or potatoes will have an unpleasant, pastelike consistency. You may have to puree soup in two or more steps, depending on the capacity of your processor. Transfer soup to a bowl or tureen and stir in cream and seasonings. Chill. Garnish with chopped chives or scallions before serving.

**Serves:** 6 to 8

# Mexican Black Bean Soup

*In Mexico, dinner is not considered a proper meal unless soup is served. And dinner, which starts between one and two o'clock in the afternoon, continues for well over two hours through course after delicious course of appetizers, soup, fish, salad, roast, and dessert. After a large bowl of soup, the tendency for this American is to stop eating—but one mustn't insult the host and hostess!*

**1 pound black beans, presoaked and drained**
**6 cups water**
**1 pound lean pork, trimmed and cubed**
**1 tablespoon oil**
**2 onions, peeled and cut into quarters**
**2 cloves garlic, peeled**
**2 tomatoes, peeled and halved**
**1 green pepper, seeded and cut into 4 pieces**
**¼ teaspoon ground cumin**
**¼ teaspoon thyme**
**⅛ teaspoon chili pepper**
**Salt and freshly ground black pepper to taste**
**Fresh lime slices**

Place beans in a large kettle with water and bring slowly to a boil. Fry pork cubes in oil until brown and add to bean pot.

Place metal blade in food processor. Add onions, garlic, tomatoes, and green pepper to processor and chop. Add vegetable mixture and seasonings to bean pot and cook approximately 4 hours, or until beans and pork cubes are tender.

Puree bean soup in food processor, using metal blade. You may have to do this in two or more steps, depending on the capacity of your processor. Correct seasoning. Heat soup until it is piping hot and serve with lime slices.

**Serves:** 6 to 8

# Harry's Perfect Gazpacho

*There are many recipes for this cold Spanish soup, but this is my husband's very own version. It is the result of his search for the* perfect *gazpacho, and many of our friends think he has found it.*

**3 cloves garlic, peeled**
**1 medium onion, peeled and quartered**
**1 cucumber, peeled and cut into 4 pieces**
**3 ripe tomatoes, peeled and cut into halves**
**1 green pepper, seeded and cut into 4 pieces**
**Salt to taste**
**Dash of cayenne pepper**
**¼ cup wine vinegar**
**¼ cup olive oil**
**¾ cup tomato juice**
**Ground cumin to taste**
**Freshly ground black pepper to taste**

**GARNISH**

**1 cup croutons**
**3 tablespoons olive oil**
**1 garlic clove, peeled and cut in half**
**1 cucumber**
**1 onion, peeled**
**1 green pepper, seeded**

Place metal blade in food processor. Add garlic, onion, cucumber, tomatoes, and green pepper to processor and puree. Add remaining ingredients and blend mixture completely. You may have to do this in two or more steps, depending on the capacity of your processor. Pour soup into a bowl or your favorite marmite and chill.

Before serving, sauté croutons in olive oil in which you are also sautéeing garlic halves. Using metal blade, coarsely chop cucumber, onion, and green pepper in food processor and pass in separate bowls when serving the soup.

**Serves:** 8 to 10

# Hearty Lentil 'n' Sausage Soup

**2 carrots, cleaned, scraped, and each cut into 2 or 3 pieces**
**2 stalks celery, each cut into 2 or 3 pieces**
**2 medium onions, peeled and cut into quarters**
**6 or 7 sprigs Italian parsley**
**4 tablespoons vegetable oil or rendered bacon drippings**
**2 tablespoons all-purpose flour**
**6 cups hot chicken or beef broth**
**¼ teaspoon thyme**
**1½ cups washed lentils, presoaked and drained**
**Salt and freshly ground black pepper to taste**
**½ pound of cooked Polish Kielbasa sausage, cut into ½-inch rounds**

Place metal blade in food processor. Add carrots, celery, onions, and parsley to processor and chop. Heat oil or bacon drippings in a 5-quart pot and sauté vegetables until they're translucent and barely tender. Stir in flour and cook for 2 to 3 minutes over low heat, stirring constantly. Slowly pour in hot chicken or beef broth, stirring steadily so that flour and broth are well blended. Bring mixture to a simmer and add all remaining ingredients except sausage. Cover pot and cook approximately two hours or until lentils are completely cooked.

Pour soup into food processor and, using metal blade, puree. You may have to do this in two or more steps, depending on the capacity of your processor. Pour soup back into pot, add sausage, and heat thoroughly. Serve with pumpernickel or black bread.

**Serves:** 6 to 8

# Aunt Vicenza's Minestrone

**¼ pound salt pork, cut into 3 pieces**
**1 clove garlic, peeled**
**1 small onion, peeled and cut in half**
**5 sprigs Italian parsley**
**2 stalks celery, each cut into 2 pieces**
**2 carrots, cleaned, scraped, and each cut into 3 pieces**
**¼ cup olive oil**
**2 tablespoons tomato paste**
**6 cups chicken or beef broth**
**2 potatoes, each peeled and cut in half**
**2 zucchini, each peeled and cut in half**
**1 cup cooked chick peas**
**Salt and freshly ground black pepper to taste**
**1 cup small shell pasta**
**Freshly grated Parmesan cheese**

Place metal blade in food processor. Add salt pork, garlic, onion, parsley, celery, and carrots to processor. Chop. Place olive oil in a large soup pot, heat gently, and add all ingredients from processor. Cook until slightly brown. Stir in tomato paste and add ½ cup of broth. Cook 5 minutes. Using metal blade, chop potatoes and then zucchini and add to soup pot. Add chick peas, remainder of broth, and salt and pepper. Cook 30 to 40 minutes, until vegetables are completely tender. Add pasta and cook until shells are firmly cooked, or *al dente,* approximately 8 to 10 minutes. Correct seasoning. Serve with grated cheese.

**Serves:** 6 to 8

# Shrimp Bisque

**2 stalks celery, each cut in half**
**2 carrots, cleaned, scraped, and each cut into 3 pieces**
**2 onions, peeled and each cut in half**
**4 sprigs parsley**
**1 clove garlic, peeled**
**1 pound mushrooms**
**1 tablespoon vegetable oil**
**2 tablespoons butter**
**1 pound raw shrimp, cleaned and deveined**
**1 sixteen-ounce can stewed tomatoes**
**2 cups chicken or fish broth**
**½ cup dry white wine**
**2 tablespoons brandy**
**¼ teaspoon dried basil**
**1 sprig fresh dill**
**¼ teaspoon white pepper**
**1 teaspoon salt**
**2 cups heavy cream**

Place metal blade in food processor. Add celery, carrots, onions, parsley, and garlic to processor and chop coarsely. Add mushrooms and process until mushrooms are coarsely chopped. Remove vegetables from processor and reserve. Heat oil and butter in a 3 quart saucepan. Sauté shrimp for 3 minutes, stirring. Add chopped vegetables and sauté an additional 2 minutes. Add all remaining ingredients, except cream, to saucepan. Bring mixture to a boil. Lower heat and simmer for 1 hour.

Using metal blade, puree soup. Depending on size of your processor bowl, you may have to do this in two steps. Return pureed soup to saucepan and simmer 10 minutes or until hot. Remove from heat and stir in cream.

**Serves:** 8 to 10

# SAUCES AND SALAD DRESSINGS

A sauce or flavorful salad dressing goes a long way in telling family and friends that you have made something special just for them. And while bottled sauces and dressings are readily available, they have none of the extra flavor that is offered by a brown sauce or a garlic mayonnaise made in your own kitchen.

In the past, preparing a homemade sauce took time, too much time for anyone involved in events outside of the kitchen. Now the food processor has taken the drudgery out of making your own sauces. The processor will chop onions, garlic cloves, and tomatoes in seconds and blend homemade mayonnaise to create a variety of flavored salad dressings. Not too long ago, a French garlicky *rouille* sauce or an Italian *pesto* called for pounding in a mortar with a pestle. Today, the food processor makes quick work of these and many other tasks.

Sauces and homemade dressings liven up the simplest meal. Tuna, taken from the can, drained, and topped with a dollop of mayonnaise you made yourself, is no longer pedestrian tuna salad. And an inexpensive cut of meat used for boiled beef takes on extra grace notes when served with your own Fresh Horseradish Cream Sauce.

# Mayonnaise

*Homemade mayonnaise should be prepared in small batches since, unlike the store-bought variety, it contains no preservatives. You should plan to use it within five days.*

## I

**1 egg**
**1 teaspoon dry mustard**
**1 tablespoon wine vinegar**
**½ teaspoon salt**
**¼ teaspoon lemon pepper**
**1 cup vegetable oil**

Place metal blade in food processor. Add all ingredients, except oil, to processor. Process for about 10 seconds, or until combined. Add oil slowly to processor through feed tube in a steady stream. Mixture will begin to thicken in 1 minute.

**Yield:** Approximately 1 cup

## II

**2 egg yolks**
**¼ teaspoon salt**
**2 teaspoons Dijon mustard**
**3 teaspoons lemon juice**
**1 cup olive oil**

Place metal blade in food processor. Add all ingredients except oil to processor and process for about 10 seconds, or until combined. Add oil slowly to the processor through feed tube in a steady stream. Mixture will begin to thicken. Because this recipe calls for 2 egg yolks, you may find that this mayonnaise thickens more quickly than the preceding recipe.

**Yield:** Approximately 1½ cups

## III

**2 egg yolks**
**1 egg**
**½ teaspoon Dijon mustard**
**¼ teaspoon salt**
**2 teaspoons lemon juice**
**1 cup olive oil**
**1 cup salad oil**
**Freshly ground white pepper to taste**

Place metal blade in food processor. Add egg yolks, egg, mustard, and salt to processor. Process for about 10 seconds, or until combined. Add lemon juice and oil slowly through feed tube in a steady stream. Check flavor of mayonnaise after adding half the oil and correct seasoning. Add salad oil and continue processing until mixture thickens.

**Yield:** Approximately 2½ cups

# Cucumber Dill Sauce

**1 small cucumber, peeled**
**½ cup homemade Mayonnaise (see pages 60–61)**
**2 teaspoons lemon juice**
**6 sprigs fresh dill, chopped**
**Salt and freshly ground white pepper to taste**

Place shredding disc in food processor. Shred cucumber (you should have about ½ cup). Drain and place in bowl. Add all other ingredients to cucumber; stir to combine. Serve with fried fish or cold boiled shrimp.

**Yield:** Approximately 1 cup

# Tartar Sauce

**2 tiny, sweet gherkin pickles**
**1 scallion or green onion**
**2 sprigs parsley**
**1 cup homemade Mayonnaise (see pages 60–61)**
**1 tablespoon capers**

Place metal blade in food processor. Add pickles, scallion, and parsley to processor and chop coarsely. Add mayonnaise and capers to processor and process until all ingredients are blended.

**Yield:** Approximately 1½ cups

# Herb Mayonnaise

**1 egg**
**1 teaspoon dry mustard**
**1 tablespoon wine vinegar**
**½ teaspoon salt**
**¼ teaspoon lemon pepper**
**1 cup vegetable oil**
**½ cup Italian parsley or basil or ½ cup combination of both**

Place metal blade in food processor. Add egg, mustard, vinegar, salt, and lemon pepper to processor, and process for about 10 seconds. Add oil gradually and slowly through feed tube until mixture begins to thicken. Add parsley, or parsley-basil mixture, to processor and process for an additional 30 seconds.

**Yield:** Approximately 1 cup

# Aioli

Aioli *is a staple in most French kitchens, but it comes as a happy surprise to most Americans who have never thought of combining mayonnaise and garlic. The French use* aioli *in a variety of ways, from adding it to fish soups to make them more garlicky, to spreading it on cold meats that are frequently served for Sunday suppers.* Aioli *is a useful mayonnaise to keep in the refrigerator; a few dabs can bring leftovers to life again.*

**4 cloves garlic, peeled**
**1 egg**
**1 teaspoon dry mustard**
**1 tablespoon wine vinegar**
**½ teaspoon salt**
**¼ teaspoon lemon pepper**
**1 cup olive oil**

Place metal blade in food processor. With machine on, drop garlic into processor through feed tube, and chop. Scrape down sides of bowl and add all ingredients except oil to processor. Process for about 10 seconds. Add oil gradually and slowly through feed tube and process until mixture thickens, about 30 seconds.

**Yield:** Approximately 1 cup.

# Sauce Rémoulade

**1 clove garlic, peeled**
**2 rolled fillets of anchovies with capers**
**4 sprigs herbs (may be parsley, or parsley and chives, or parsley and fresh tarragon)**
**1 hard-boiled egg, peeled and cut in half**
**1 teaspoon Dijon mustard**
**2 cups homemade Mayonnaise (see pages 60–61)**

Place metal blade in food processor. Add garlic, anchovies, herbs, egg, and mustard to processor and chop, pulsing on and off, until ingredients are chopped and combined. Spoon mixture into mayonnaise. Stir to combine thoroughly. This sauce is particularly good with fish or hard-boiled eggs.

**Yield:** Approximately 2½ cups

# Sweet Walnut Sauce with Egg Noodles

**1 cup shelled walnuts**
**4 tablespoons sugar, or more, to taste**
**2 cups sour cream**
**1 pound broad egg noodles, cooked *al dente*, drained**
**4 tablespoons butter, melted**

Place metal blade in food processor. Add nuts to processor and chop coarsely, pulsing on and off once or twice. Add sugar and sour cream to processor and process only until ingredients are combined. Do not overprocess, or nuts will be too finely chopped. Heat cooked egg noodles in butter. Top with Sweet Walnut Sauce and heat over a low flame, stirring, for 30 seconds.

**Serves:** 4 to 5

# Green Goddess Salad Dressing

**6 fillets of anchovies**
**3 scallions, each cut into 3 pieces**
**6 sprigs Italian parsley**
**8 blades fresh chives**
**½ teaspoon dried tarragon**
**2 cups homemade Mayonnaise (see pages 60–61)**
**2 tablespoons tarragon vinegar**

Place metal blade in food processor. Add anchovies, scallions, parsley, chives, and tarragon to processor and chop finely. Add mayonnaise and blend. Spoon salad dressing into a bowl and stir in vinegar.

**Yield:** Approximately 2½ cups

# Russian Dressing

**1 egg**
**1 teaspoon dry mustard**
**1 tablespoon wine vinegar**
**½ teaspoon salt**
**¼ teaspoon lemon pepper**
**1 cup vegetable oil**
**2 tablespoons catsup**
**2 tablespoons sweet relish**

Place metal blade in food processor. Add first 5 ingredients to processor and blend for about 10 seconds. Add oil slowly to processor, through feed tube, in a steady stream until mixture begins to thicken. Add the catsup and relish to the processor and continue processing for another 20 seconds.

**Yield:** Approximately 1 cup

# Roquefort Dressing

**¾ cup olive oil**
**½ teaspoon salt**
**¼ teaspoon mild paprika**
**Freshly ground black pepper to taste**
**¼ cup wine vinegar**
**3 ounces or 4 tablespoons Roquefort cheese**

Place metal blade in food processor. Add oil, salt, paprika, pepper, and vinegar to processor and blend thoroughly. Add Roquefort cheese and continue processing until mixture is thoroughly blended.

**Yield:** Approximately 1 cup

# Easy Hollandaise

**3 egg yolks**
**2 tablespoons lemon juice**
**¼ teaspoon salt**
**⅛ teaspoon freshly ground white pepper**
**¼ pound butter, melted**

Place metal blade in food processor. Add egg yolks, lemon juice, salt, and pepper to processor, and process for 2 or 3 seconds. With machine on, add butter gradually through feed tube. Mixture will thicken as it is processed. Especially recommended with asparagus or poached salmon.

**Yield:** Approximately 1 cup

# Fresh Horseradish Cream Sauce

**1 two-inch piece of fresh horseradish root, scraped and cut into 2 pieces**
**1 cup sour cream**
**Sugar to taste**
**Salt and freshly ground black pepper to taste**

Place shredding disc in food processor. Shred horseradish root. Remove shredding disc and place metal blade in food processor. Add all other ingredients and process until horseradish is finely chopped and sauce is thoroughly blended. Correct seasoning. Serve with boiled beef or smoked trout.

**Yield:** Approximately 1½ cups

# Basic Brown Sauce

*Mix brown sauce with the pan juices of roast beef or roast pork to make a rich gravy. Combine it with sautéed mushrooms to enliven fillet slices or mix with a quarter cup of white wine to serve over roasted veal or chicken. Brown sauce will keep for several weeks in your refrigerator if tightly sealed, or it may be frozen for future use.*

**1 carrot, cleaned, scraped, and cut into 3 or 4 pieces**
**1 small onion, peeled and cut in half**
**1 stalk celery, cut into 2 or 3 pieces**
**¼ pound butter**
**4 tablespoons all-purpose flour**
**1 tablespoon tomato paste**
**4 sprigs parsley**
**½ bay leaf**
**¼ teaspoon thyme**
**6 cups beef broth**

Place metal blade in food processor. Add carrot, onion, and celery pieces to processor and chop. Heat half the butter in a large skillet, add chopped vegetables, and sauté until tender. Meanwhile, melt remainder of butter in a large saucepan over low heat, stir in flour, and cook until flour is a tan color. When flour is tan, remove from heat. Stir in tomato paste and add chopped vegetables and the butter they have sautéed in. Add herbs and broth and stir thoroughly to prevent flour from lumping. Place over low heat, bring to a simmer, and cook for 1 hour. If sauce is too thick, you can add more beef broth or ½ cup dry vermouth. If sauce is too thin, increase heat and cook until sauce is reduced. Allow sauce to cool.

Pour sauce into food processor and blend thoroughly. You may have to do this in two or more steps, depending on the capacity of your processor. Return sauce to saucepan. Bring to simmer one more time and remove from heat. Serve immediately or refrigerate for future use.

**Yield:** Approximately 3 cups

# Rouille

*In France,* rouille *is the traditional sauce served with bouilla-baisse. It can also be served with a fish stew, and if you're a real* rouille *lover, you might enjoy it as a piquant sauce for baked fish fillets.*

**3 canned red pimientos**
**¼ teaspoon Tabasco**
**1 medium boiled potato, peeled**
**3 cloves garlic, peeled**
**4 or 5 fresh basil leaves, or 1 teaspoon dry basil**
**Salt and freshly ground black pepper to taste**
**½ cup olive oil**

Place metal blade in food processor. Add all ingredients, except oil, to food processor. Puree thoroughly. Add olive oil through feed tube in a slow but steady stream; process until thick and blended. Correct seasoning. If sauce is too thick, blend in 2 or 3 tablespoons hot water.

**Yield:** Approximately 1 cup

# Easy Tomato Sauce

**1 six-ounce can tomato paste**
**2 cups canned whole stewed tomatoes**
**1 stalk celery, cut into 3 pieces**
**1 clove garlic, peeled**
**1 small onion, peeled and cut in half**
**Sugar to taste**
**Salt to taste**
**¼ teaspoon hot red pepper flakes (optional)**

Place metal blade in food processor. Add all ingredients to processor and blend thoroughly. Correct seasoning and pour sauce into a heavy saucepan. Cook over low heat for 30 minutes. This is delicious over meat loaf, chicken, or baked fish fillets.

**Yield:** Approximately 2½ cups

# Italian-Style Tomato Sauce

**1 medium onion, peeled**
**2 cloves garlic, peeled**
**2 tablespoons olive oil**
**1 sixteen-ounce can Italian-style plum tomatoes**
**½ cup fresh basil leaves**
**¼ teaspoon oregano**
**½ teaspoon sugar**
**Salt and freshly ground black pepper to taste**

Place metal blade in food processor. Add onion and garlic to processor and chop. Heat oil in a large skillet. Sauté onion-garlic mixture until translucent.

Place all other ingredients in processor and, using metal blade, chop and blend. Add to skillet. Cover and cook, stirring from time to time, until sauce has reduced and thickened.

**Yield:** Approximately 2 cups

# Pesto

Pesto *can be made only with fresh basil, and unfortunately the basil season is short. However, you can prepare the sauce (eliminating the cheese and butter) and freeze it for later use. When you are ready to use it, just defrost, add the cheese and butter, and serve over pasta.* Pesto *is especially fine on fettuccine, cooked* al dente, *of course.*

**2 firmly packed cups of basil leaves**
**½ cup olive oil**
**2 tablespoons pine, or pignolia, nuts**
**2 cloves garlic, peeled and each clove cut in half**
**1 teaspoon salt**
**½ cup freshly grated Parmesan cheese**
**3 tablespoons butter, cut into 2 or 3 pieces**

Place metal blade in food processor. Add basil, oil, nuts, garlic, and salt to processor and puree thoroughly. Add cheese and continue blending. Add butter and blend once again. Place *pesto* sauce in a bowl and, before serving with pasta, stir in 2 tablespoons of the hot water in which the pasta has cooked.

**Yield:** Sauce for 4 servings of pasta

# Peachy Barbecue Sauce

**1 medium onion, peeled and cut in half**
**1 clove garlic, peeled**
**3 sprigs Italian parsley**
**Pulp of ½ lemon that has been seeded**
**1 six-ounce can tomato paste**
**¼ cup wine vinegar**
**½ cup water**
**¼ cup salad oil**
**2 teaspoons dry mustard**
**1 teaspoon soy sauce**
**1 teaspoon salt**
**1 tablespoon chili powder**
**1 tablespoon brown sugar**
**1 four-and-three-quarter-ounce jar strained baby peaches**

Place metal biade in food processor. Add first 4 ingredients to processor and chop. Add remaining ingredients and process until smooth.

**Yield:** Approximately 2 cups

# Spicy Barbecue Sauce

**1 small onion, peeled and cut in half**
**1 clove garlic, peeled**
**⅓ cup vegetable oil**
**2 ripe tomatoes, peeled and halved**
**4 tablespoons chili powder**
**1 cup light molasses**
**½ cup cider vinegar**
**1 tablespoon Worcestershire sauce**
**½ teaspoon Tabasco**
**1 teaspoon mustard**
**4 teaspoons salt**
**1 tablespoon oregano**
**2 cups water**

Place metal blade in food processor. Add onion and garlic to processor and chop. Heat oil in a large saucepan and sauté onion and garlic until translucent. Place tomatoes in food processor and chop. Add to onion-garlic mixture and cook an additional 5 minutes, stirring. Add all remaining ingredients; stir to blend. Bring mixture to a boil. Lower heat and simmer uncovered for 20 to 30 minutes.

**Yield:** Approximately 1 quart

# Raita

Raita *is an East Indian favorite and is marvelous when served with shish kebab or Lamb Kofta Kebabs (for recipe, see page 110). It's also excellent as a dip when served with pappadums, the East Indian fried wafers.*

**1 cucumber, peeled**
**1 small onion, peeled**
**2 cups yogurt**
**1 teaspoon ground cumin**
**Salt and freshly ground white pepper to taste**

Place shredding disc in food processor. Shred cucumber and onion.

Remove shredding disc and place plastic blade in processor. Add all other ingredients and process until mixture is thoroughly blended. Spoon into a bowl and chill for 1 hour before serving.

**Yield:** Approximately 2 cups

# White Clam Sauce

**2 dozen littleneck clams**
**½ small onion, peeled**
**4 cloves garlic, peeled**
**¼ cup fresh parsley**
**½ cup olive oil**
**¼ teaspoon hot red pepper flakes**
**¼ cup dry white wine**
**1 tablespoon butter, softened**
**2 tablespoons freshly grated Parmesan cheese**
**Salt to taste**

Wash and scrub the clams. Clams can be opened more easily if they are placed for about 10 minutes in freezer, then removed and opened with a clam knife. If they are still difficult to open, place them in a covered saucepan with a small amount of water in bottom of the pan. Heat until clams open up and remove from shells and place in a bowl. Discard shells. Reserve clam juices. Place metal blade in food processor. Add clams. Pulse on and off until clams are just chopped. Remove and reserve. With motor running, drop onion and garlic through feed tube and process until just chopped. Add parsley to processor. Pulse on and off until chopped.

Heat oil in a saucepan. Add onion, garlic, and parsley and sauté for 2 to 3 minutes. Add hot pepper and wine. Cook until sauce reduces by half, about 5 minutes.

Strain clam juice through a sieve lined with paper towels. You should have about ⅔ cup liquid. Add clam juices to sauce and cook quickly, until sauce is reduced by half. Add the clams to the sauce, stirring to combine, and remove from heat. Stir in butter and cheese, and salt, if needed. Pour over linguine, cooked *al dente,* and serve.

**Serves:** 4

# Berry Mayonnaise

**1 egg**
**1 tablespoon lemon juice**
**1½ teaspoons vinegar**
**½ teaspoon salt**
**¾ cup oil**
**1 tablespoon sugar**
**1 pint fresh or frozen raspberries or strawberries or 1 eight-ounce can cranberry sauce**

Place metal blade in food processor. Add egg, lemon juice, vinegar, and salt. Process 10 seconds. Pour oil slowly through feed tube in a steady stream. Mixture will begin to thicken. When mayonnaise is thick, add sugar and half the berries (if using frozen berries, defrost first). Process 10 seconds. Turn into a bowl, fold in remaining berries. Serve over fresh fruit.

**Yield:** 2 cups

# PÂTÉS

If you can make a meat loaf, then you can make a pâté or terrine—with a food processor. The problem of preparing pâtés in the past was finding a butcher willing to grind pork, pork fat, and veal in his machine. Now, with the help of a food processor, homemade pâtés can become a regular feature at your table, and they can be as simple or as elaborate as you wish.

Today there is no difference between a pâté and a terrine. Originally a pâté was a meat mixture baked in a crust; a terrine was the same mixture baked in a terrine, or earthenware dish. The terms *pâté* and *terrine* now are used interchangeably.

Pâtés are a delight to take along on a picnic, can be enjoyed as a first course, or can be served as a main course with tiny *cornichon* pickles, sliced tomatoes, and a bottle of robust Beaujolais wine.

# Chicken Liver Pâté en Croûte

**1 pound chicken livers, washed, dried, and cut in half**
**2 eggs**
**1 tablespoon cognac**
**¾ cup heavy sweet cream**
**1 small onion, peeled and cut in half**
**¼ cup all-purpose flour**
**2 teaspoons salt**
**½ teaspoon ground ginger**
**1 teaspoon white pepper**
**½ teaspoon allspice**
**Pâté Brisée II recipe (see page 202)**
**1 egg, beaten**

Place metal blade in food processor. Add half of livers and eggs, cognac, and cream to processor. Pulse on and off once or twice. Scrape down sides of bowl and add remainder of livers, onion, and flour. Process until mixture is smooth and ingredients are combined. Add salt and spices and process until incorporated into mixture. Roll out Pâté Brisée II dough and line a buttered pan that is approximately 15¾×2¼×2¾ inches. Spoon chicken liver puree into pan and fold dough over to cover the puree.

Make rosettes of scraps of dough and decorate the center of the pâté. Pierce each rosette with a sharp knife and prick casing with a fork at the edge of the pâté.

Brush dough with beaten egg and bake in a preheated 350-degree oven for approximately 45 minutes or until dough is brown.

**Serves:** 8

# Harry's Chicken Liver Pâté

*This is my husband's recipe for the ultimate chicken liver pâté. As you can see, there are few ingredients, and the result is a pâté with the richest flavor of chicken liver.*

**1 pound chicken livers**
**1 cup, or more, rendered chicken fat**
**1 large onion, peeled and cut into quarters**
**Salt and freshly ground black pepper to taste**

Wash chicken livers. Cut in half and, while doing so, remove all visible bits of vein or gristle. Pat chicken livers dry with paper towels. Heat chicken fat in a large skillet. Place chicken livers in skillet and sauté until they are firm but pink inside. Place metal blade in food processor. Add livers and juices from skillet to processor. Add onion and process, pulsing machine on and off and scraping down sides of bowl, until pâté mixture is a smooth blend. You may have to do this in two steps, depending on size of your processor bowl. Season to taste, add more chicken fat if you wish, and pulse on and off once more. Spoon chicken liver pâté into a 4-cup terrine and decorate with sliced red radishes. Chill at least 4 hours, or overnight. Serve with fresh rye bread and paper-thin onion slices.

**Serves:** 6 to 8

# Pâté of Chicken and Goose Liver with Mushrooms and Ham

**3 tablespoons rendered goose fat, if available, or butter**
**1 cup mushrooms**
**1 small onion, peeled and cut in half**
**½ pound chicken livers, cut in half**
**1 large goose liver, cut into 4 pieces**
**¼ cup chicken broth**
**½ pound boiled ham, cut into cubes or large strips**
**Salt and freshly ground black pepper to taste**

Heat goose fat or butter in a large skillet. Place metal blade in food processor and add mushrooms and onion to processor. Chop coarsely. Add chicken and goose livers and mushroom-onion mixture to skillet. Sauté briefly, stirring, until livers have lost their pink color. Spoon all ingredients from skillet into processor. Add chicken stock and ham. Process, pulsing on and off and scraping down sides of bowl, until mixture is thoroughly smooth and blended. Season and pulse on and off once again. Oil a 3-cup terrine. Spoon pâté into terrine and refrigerate several hours or overnight. Pâté may be unmolded or served directly from terrine. If you wish, decorate with slices of hard-cooked eggs, chopped scallion, and parsley.

**Serves:** 6 to 8

# Chicken Pâté Romanoff

**1 shallot, peeled**
**1 clove garlic, peeled**
**4 tablespoons butter**
**1 pound veal, boned, trimmed, and cut into cubes**
**5 chicken legs, skinned and boned, the meat cut into pieces**
**1½ cups homemade bread crumbs**
**1 egg**
**½ tablespoon mild paprika**
**½ teaspoon Herbes de Provence (or ¼ teaspoon thyme and ¼ bay leaf, crushed)**
**3 tablespoons Italian parsley**
**½ cup dry white wine**
**¼ cup brandy**

Place metal blade in food processor. With machine on, drop shallot and garlic through feed tube and chop. Remove from processor and sauté in butter until translucent. Return shallot, garlic, and butter in which they were sautéed to processor. Add all other ingredients to processor and grind and blend thoroughly. It may be necessary to do this in two steps depending upon the size of your processor bowl. Spoon pâté mixture into a buttered 5-cup terrine or loaf pan. Set pan in a larger one that's partially filled with water and bake in a preheated 350-degree oven for 1 hour and 30 minutes.

**Serves:** 8 to 10

# Veal and Chicken Pâté en Croûte

**¾ pound boneless veal, trimmed and cut into cubes**
**¾ pound breast of boned, skinned chicken, cut into cubes**
**½ cup homemade bread crumbs**
**1 egg**
**¼ cup heavy sweet cream**
**2 tablespoons dry sherry**
**¼ pound mushrooms**
**¼ teaspoon tarragon**
**3 sprigs parsley**
**1 tablespoon fresh, or dried, chives**
**½ teaspoon salt**
**Pâté Brisée I (see page 201)**
**1 beaten egg**

Place metal blade in food processor. Add veal and chicken to processor and grind. Pulse machine on and off and scrape down sides of bowl. When meat is ground, add all other ingredients, except for pâté brisée and beaten egg, to processor. Process, blending all ingredients thoroughly. You may have to do this in two steps, depending upon size of your processor bowl.

Spoon meat mixture into a buttered 8½×4½×2½-inch loaf pan. Bake in a preheated 350-degree oven for 1 hour. Allow meat mixture to cool and then remove from pan.

Make pâté brisée according to directions on page 201. Roll out the dough and place cooled loaf in center. Fold dough over the meat to cover it completely. Tuck in dough at the edges. Place seam side down on a baking sheet. Make rosettes out of scraps of dough and decorate the center of the pâté. Pierce each rosette with a sharp knife and prick dough casing with a fork at the edges of the pâté. Brush dough with beaten egg and bake in a preheated 400-degree oven for approximately 40 minutes or until crust is brown.

**Serves:** 8

# Country-Style Terrine from Au Relais Hostellerie

*It was our good fortune to be taken through the château country of France's Loire Valley by our French friends Batia, Arthur, Raymonde, and Theo. Along the way, we stopped at a small country inn, Au Relais Hostellerie, in Bracieux, where we had a meal that the resident of any castle might have envied. The first course was a terrine, which the owner and chef of this marvelous inn described as "the usual country-style pâte—nothing special." It tasted very special to us, and I think it will to you, too.*

**½ pound boned, trimmed pork, cut into cubes**
**½ pound fresh pork fat, cut into pieces**
**½ pound breast of boned, skinned chicken, cut into cubes**
**Salt and freshly ground black pepper to taste**
**½ teaspoon thyme**
**2 cloves garlic, peeled**
**1 small onion, peeled**
**4 tablespoons cognac**
**2 eggs**
**½ pound pork liver, cut into large chunks**
**Sheets of fresh pork fat, about ⅛ inch thick, to line terrine**

Place metal blade in food processor. Add pork, pork fat, chicken, salt, pepper, thyme, garlic, and onions to processor and grind. Add cognac and eggs and continue blending. You may have to do this in two or more steps, depending on the capacity of your processor. Sauté a tablespoonful of mixture in a skillet; taste and correct seasoning. Spoon mixture into a large bowl. Place pork liver in food processor and chop coarsely. Stir chopped pork liver into mixture in bowl. Line bottom and sides of a 6-cup terrine or loaf pan with sheets of pork fat and spoon mixture into terrine. Cover mixture with another sheet of pork fat. Make sure that the fat is tucked in on sides and at the ends so mixture is completely covered. Seal the entire pan with foil. Set terrine in a larger pan of water and place in a preheated oven of 350 degrees. Bake approximately 2 hours. Pâté is cooked when meat shrinks from sides of terrine or loaf pan in which it is cooking. Test for doneness by pressing top of pâté with a spoon. There should be no traces of pink in juices. Or you can test by piercing the center with a metal skewer. Skewer should come out clean.

Remove pâté from oven. Place another pan on top of pâté and place a weight within this pan. Pâté should be weighted down as it cools so that excess fat is pressed out and pâté is easier to slice. When pâté has cooled, refrigerate, with the weight still on. Be sure not to pour off any of the cooking juices.

Serve pâté only after it is thoroughly chilled. You may serve right from the terrine.

**Serves:** 12 to 14

# Sausage Pâté en Croûte

**1 small onion, peeled**
**3 shallots, peeled**
**2 scallions, each one cut into 3 pieces**
**6 slices bacon**
**2 pounds pork sausage meat**
**3 eggs**
**3 cups homemade bread crumbs**
**Salt and freshly ground black pepper to taste**
**¼ teaspoon thyme**
**2 tablespoons cognac**
**All-American Piecrust Dough (see page 204, and double the recipe)**
**1 beaten egg**

Place metal blade in food processor. Add onion, shallots, and scallions to processor and chop. Leave vegetables in processor. In a large skillet fry the bacon. When bacon is crisp, remove from heat and combine with sausage meat. Add bacon, sausage meat, eggs, and bread crumbs to food processor. Blend thoroughly. You may have to do this in two or more steps, depending on the capacity of your processor. Season sausage mixture, add cognac, and sauté a tablespoon of mixture in a skillet. Taste, and correct seasoning. Line a 5-cup terrine or loaf pan with rolled-out piecrust dough. Spoon mixture into terrine, bringing pie crust dough over top of sausage mixture. Brush with beaten egg. Bake terrine in a preheated 350-degree oven for 45 minutes. Invert pan on a flat plate and refrigerate overnight. Slide loaf from pan the following day.

**Serves:** 8

# Jellied Ham Pâté

**3 shallots, peeled and minced**
**2 tablespoons sweet butter**
**1 cup chicken broth**
**1 canned pimiento**
**1 stalk celery, cut into 2 pieces**
**½ green pepper, cut into 2 pieces**
**¼ pound boiled ham, cut into cubes or strips**
**1 teaspoon Dijon mustard**
**2 tablespoons tomato paste**
**2 tablespoons cognac**
**1 envelope unflavored gelatin softened in 2 tablespoons dry vermouth**
**Salt and freshly ground black pepper to taste**
**½ cup heavy sweet cream, whipped**

Place shallots and butter in a saucepan and cook until shallots are translucent. Stir in chicken broth, bring to a simmer, and reserve. Place metal blade in food processor. Add pimiento, celery, green pepper, and ham to processor and process until all ingredients are finely chopped and blended. You may have to do this in two or more steps, depending on the capacity of your processor. Add shallot-chicken broth mixture, mustard, tomato paste, and cognac to processor and blend thoroughly. Add gelatin-wine mixture to processor and blend thoroughly. Spoon mixture from processor into a large bowl and add seasonings. Fold in whipped cream and spoon pâté into a 4-cup buttered mold. Chill overnight or until set.

**Serves:** 6

# MEATS

If you like Steak Tartare, freshly ground meat for hamburgers, and a wonderful hash made from leftovers, you'll love the food processor—and the recipes in this section. The old meat grinder was a nuisance to work and an even greater nuisance to keep clean, but now you can grind meat easily in the processor, and because you're doing it yourself, you'll know that it's truly fresh.

Most butchers are reluctant to chop anything other than beef in their grinders. With your own food processor you can easily prepare meat loaves and meatballs made with chopped pork and veal and Middle Eastern dishes made with chopped lamb. And when you grind your own meats, you can be absolutely certain of the contents of every dish you prepare.

The food processor also solves the leftovers problem. Instead of shifting yesterday's turkey or roast beef from one refrigerator shelf to another, you can grind the meat in the processor and combine it with vegetables or a freshly prepared sauce to create new and exciting meals.

# Vitello Tonnato

Vitello Tonnato *has long been a favorite among people who like fine Italian food, but many preferred to eat it in restaurants rather than prepare it at home. It simply took too much time and trouble to puree the Tuna Sauce through a sieve or strainer. It's no trouble now, thanks to the food processor.*

*Serve* Vitello Tonnato *with a first course of small black olives, pimientos, slices of mortadella, and crisp, thin bread sticks. Prepare a romaine and escarole salad and serve a dry white Italian wine.*

**2 tablespoons olive oil**
**3 pounds boneless rolled leg of veal**
**1 large onion, peeled and cut into quarters**
**2 carrots, cleaned, scraped, and each one cut into 3 pieces**
**3 stalks celery, each one cut into 2 pieces**
**2 cloves garlic, peeled**
**3 sprigs Italian parsley**
**1 two-ounce can anchovy fillets**
**1 seven-ounce can tuna fish, drained**
**1 cup dry white wine**
**1 cup chicken broth**
**¼ teaspoon oregano**
**Salt and freshly ground black pepper to taste**
**1 cup homemade Mayonnaise (see pages 60–61)**
**1 tablespoon lemon juice, or more, to taste**

Heat oil in a large Dutch oven (or a large casserole) and brown veal lightly on all sides. Place metal blade in food processor. Add onion, carrots, celery, garlic, and parsley to processor and chop. Add to veal along with anchovy, tuna, wine, broth, oregano, and salt and pepper. Cover Dutch oven and cook for 1½ to 2 hours or until veal is tender. Remove meat from Dutch oven and chill.

Cook sauce to reduce by one half, and return to food processor. Using metal blade, blend thoroughly. Chill sauce, stir in mayonnaise, and add lemon juice to taste.

When veal is chilled, cut into thin slices and serve with the sauce.

**Serves:** 6 to 8

# Beef Wellington

*Fillet of beef, rolled in a pastry crust, is a most impressive dinner or party dish. Some cooks use a many-layered puff pastry or a brioche dough for beef Wellington, but a Pâté Brisée made without sugar turns out a delicious crust.*

**Pâté Brisée II (double the recipe on page 202)**
**1 two-and-a-half- to three-pound fillet of beef**
**3 tablespoons cognac**
**Salt and freshly ground black pepper to taste**
**8 strips bacon**
**½ pound Chicken Liver Pâté (one half the recipe on page 83)**
**1 egg, beaten**

Prepare Pâté Brisée II, doubling the recipe on page 202. Depending on the capacity of your processor, you may have to do this in two steps. Chill dough for 30 to 45 minutes before using.

Preheat oven to 450 degrees. Rub the fillet with the cognac, season with salt and pepper, and place fillet in a roasting pan. Place bacon strips over top of meat. Roast fillet for 15 minutes. Remove fillet from oven. Discard bacon and allow meat to cool to room temperature. Spread Chicken Liver Pâté over fillet.

Preheat oven to 425 degrees. Roll out Pâté Brisée dough and place fillet in the center. Draw dough up from both sides so that it overlaps and tuck in ends of dough envelope-fashion, trimming off excess dough. Seal all pastry seams with beaten egg and place pastry-wrapped fillet on a baking sheet, seam side down. Brush top and sides of fillet with remaining beaten egg. Make rosettes out of dough scraps and decorate top of fillet with rosettes. Pierce center of each rosette with a sharp knife and prick pastry casing on top and sides. Place fillet in oven and bake for approximately 30 minutes or until pastry is cooked and has browned.

**Serves:** 6 to 8

# Meat Loaf

**1 pound beef, trimmed and cut into cubes**
**3 slices white bread, halved, crusts trimmed**
**1 eight-ounce can stewed tomatoes**
**1 egg**
**1 teaspoon salt**
**1 envelope dry onion soup mix**
**½ teaspoon freshly ground black pepper**
**2 sprigs parsley**
**2 slices American cheese**
**4 slices bacon**

Place metal blade in food processor. Add beef to processor and grind. Add all other ingredients, except cheese and bacon, to processor. Combine thoroughly.

Form one half of meat mixture into a loaf. Place cheese slices on top of meat. Cover cheese with remaining meat mixture, making sure that cheese is completely sealed in at the sides. Top meat mixture with bacon strips. Place meat loaf in the center of a shallow roasting pan or baking dish. Preheat oven to 350 degrees and bake for 1 hour or until well browned.

**Serves:** 6

# Meat Loaf with Water Chestnuts

**1 pound beef, trimmed and cubed**
**½ pound veal, trimmed and cubed**
**½ pound lean pork, trimmed and cubed**
**2 eggs**
**2 ounces instant oatmeal**
**6 to 8 water chestnuts**
**½ green pepper, cut into 2 pieces**
**1 small onion, peeled and cut in half**
**3 tablespoons catsup**
**1 teaspoon salt**
**½ teaspoon freshly ground black pepper**

Place metal blade in food processor. Add beef to processor and grind, pulsing on and off two or three times. Add veal and pork to processor and continue grinding, pulsing on and off and scraping down sides of bowl. Do not overprocess. Depending on size of your processor bowl, you may have to grind meat in two or more steps. When meat is almost as finely ground as you would like it, add all other ingredients and process until vegetables are chopped, and all ingredients are thoroughly combined. Remove meat mixture from processor and form into a loaf shape. Place in the center of a shallow roasting pan or baking dish and bake in a preheated 350-degree oven for 1½ hours. Serve with Tomato Sauce (see pages 73–74), if you wish.

**Serves:** 8

# Home-Style Italian Meatballs

**½ pound beef, trimmed and cut into cubes**
**¼ pound pork, trimmed and cut into cubes**
**¼ pound veal, trimmed and cut into cubes**
**4 sprigs Italian parsley**
**1 egg**
**1 small onion, peeled and cut in half**
**2 cloves garlic, peeled**
**4 slices white bread, halved, crusts trimmed**
**1 teaspoon salt**
**⅛ teaspoon freshly ground black pepper**
**¼ teaspoon oregano**
**½ cup olive oil**

Place metal blade in food processor. Add beef, pork, and veal to processor and grind. Add all other ingredients, except oil, to meat, and continue processing until mixture is thoroughly mixed. This may require two or more steps, depending on the capacity of your processor. Pulse on and off as you process, scraping meat down from sides of the bowl.

When mixture is combined, form into meatballs, approximately 2 inches in diameter. Heat olive oil in a large skillet and fry meatballs until they are brown. (If you wish, instead of frying, you may cook meatballs for 1 hour in your favorite marinara sauce and serve over spaghetti.)

**Serves:** 6

# Swedish Meatballs

**½ pound beef, trimmed and cut into cubes**
**¼ pound veal, trimmed and cut into cubes**
**¼ pound pork, trimmed and cut into cubes**
**4 slices of white bread, cut in half**
**1 large onion, peeled and cut into quarters**
**4 sprigs Italian parsley**
**1 clove garlic, peeled**
**1 egg**
**1 cup sweet cream**
**1 teaspoon salt**
**4 sprigs fresh dill**
**Freshly ground black pepper to taste**
**¼ pound, or more, sweet butter**
**1 ten-and-a-half-ounce can condensed onion soup**
**½ cup water**
**¼ cup beer**
**¼ cup catsup**
**1 tablespoon all-purpose flour**
**½ cup sour cream**

Place metal blade in food processor. Add all meats to processor and grind, pulsing on and off once or twice. Add bread, onion, parsley, and garlic to processor. Scrape down sides of bowl and pulse on and off twice. Add egg, cream, salt, dill, and pepper to processor, scrape down sides of bowl, and grind until ingredients are finely ground and thoroughly combined.

Form meat mixture into meatballs approximately 2 inches in diameter. Heat butter in a large skillet and brown meatballs. Remove meatballs to another dish and add onion soup, water, beer, and catsup to skillet. Bring to a simmer. Combine flour and sour cream in a small bowl, mixing well, and add gradually to skillet. Simmer sauce for about 10 minutes. Add meatballs to skillet and heat for another 5 minutes. Serve with wide buttered egg noodles.

**Serves:** 6

# Ham Loaf in Potato Crust

**HAM LOAF**

**1½ pounds cooked ham, cut into cubes**
**½ pound Italian sausage, casing removed, cut into slices**
**2 slices canned pineapple, cut in half**
**1 tablespoon soy sauce**
**2 teaspoons Dijon mustard**
**2 eggs**
**4 slices white bread, crusts trimmed, cut into quarters**
**3 sprigs parsley**
**1 medium onion, peeled and cut in half**
**½ green pepper, seeded and cut into pieces**

**POTATO CRUST**

**1 pound potatoes, peeled, cubed, cooked, and drained**
**1 three-ounce package cream cheese, cut into 3 pieces**
**¼ pound Cheddar cheese, cut into cubes**
**2 tablespoons butter**
**2 tablespoons milk**
**1 tablespoon dried chives**
**¼ teaspoon salt**
**¼ teaspoon white pepper**
**Mild paprika**

*To Make Ham Loaf:*

Place metal blade in food processor. Place ham in food processor and grind. You may have to do this in two or more steps, depending on the capacity of your processor. Remove and reserve. Place all other ham loaf ingredients in processor and grind. Add ham to processor and blend all ingredients thoroughly. Pulse on and off and scrape mixture down from sides of bowl. You may have to do this in two or more steps. Spoon ham loaf mixture into a buttered 9×5×3-inch loaf pan. Bake in a preheated 350-degree oven for 1 hour and 15 minutes.

*To Make Potato Crust:*

Place metal blade in food processor. Add cooked potatoes and, with machine on, add cream cheese, Cheddar cheese, and butter to processor. Scrape down sides of bowl and pulse on and off. Add all remaining ingredients, except paprika, to processor and continue processing until all ingredients are combined and smooth.

Turn baked Ham Loaf onto baking sheet. Spread potato mixture over loaf. If desired, you can decorate ham loaf on top by piping part of potato mixture through a pastry tube. Sprinkle top of loaf with paprika. Bake in 400-degree oven for 20 minutes.

**Serves:** 6

# Rotisserie Flank Steak

**1 flank steak, 2 to 2½ pounds**
**Salt and freshly ground black pepper to taste**
**2 tablespoons butter**
**1 large Spanish onion, peeled and cut into 4 pieces**
**6 sprigs Italian parsley**
**1 cup dry red wine**
**¼ cup dark molasses**
**2 cloves garlic, peeled and each cut into 4 pieces**

Sprinkle flank steak with salt and pepper and set aside. Heat butter in a skillet. Place metal blade in food processor. Add onion and parsley to processor and chop. Add chopped onion and parsley to hot butter and sauté until onions are translucent. Spread flank steak with onion-parsley mixture. Starting at narrow end, roll up steak and tie with string. Skewer ends of roll to keep stuffing inside meat.

Make a marinade by combining wine, molasses, and garlic. Pour over meat, which has been placed in a glass or earthenware dish. Let stand 4 to 8 hours.

To cook: Place meat on a rotisserie skewer, making sure that it is properly balanced for easy turning. Roast meat about 6 inches from gray coals. Brush with marinade every 10 to 15 minutes. Roast for about 1 hour or until meat is tender. Remove from skewer and cut into 1-inch slices.

**Serves:** 6

# Crispy Hash Pancake

**1 pound, or more, of leftover roast beef, cut into cubes**
**1 large onion, peeled and cut into quarters**
**1 green pepper, cored, seeded, and cut into 4 pieces**
**¼ cup catsup**
**4 large Idaho potatoes, peeled, cut into cubes, and boiled**
**Salt and freshly ground black pepper to taste**

Place metal blade in food processor. Add roast beef, onion, green pepper, and catsup to processor and chop. You may have to do this in two or more steps, depending on the capacity of your processor. Remove beef mixture to a large bowl and add potatoes and seasoning; mash together with a large fork. Do not add the potatoes to the meat in the food processor, because potatoes will become finely processed and the texture of this hash will be too smooth.

Spread hash mixture in a thin layer over a lightly greased or teflon-coated baking pan or baking sheet and place in a preheated 450-degree oven. Bake until hash is very brown and crispy. Depending on your oven, this can take anywhere from 20 to 40 minutes. Serve in large wedges with a sliced tomato and onion salad.

**Serves:** 4 to 6

# Steak Tartare

*We've discovered that more people are developing a taste for raw beef. Years ago, when we served this dish, people would edge away from the table. Now we find more people heading for the platter holding the Steak Tartare. The essential ingredient in this dish is freshness. The spices and herbs can be varied to suit your taste. After you prepare the basic meat mixture, you can add extra capers, mustard, or hot sauce.*

**1 pound beef, cut into cubes (may be round, sirloin, or fillet, but must be absolutely fat-free)**
**1 whole egg**
**1 small onion, peeled and cut in half**
**2 tablespoons olive oil**
**Salt and freshly ground black pepper to taste**
**1 teaspoon Worcestershire sauce, or more, to taste**
**⅛ teaspoon Tabasco, or more, to taste**
**1 teaspoon Dijon mustard, or more, to taste**
**1 tablespoon catsup, or more, to taste**
**1 tablespoon capers**

Place metal blade in food processor. Add beef, egg, onion, and olive oil to processor. Pulse on and off twice, and scrape down sides of bowl. Add remainder of ingredients and continue processing until meat is ground and all ingredients are thoroughly combined. Remove Steak Tartare to a bowl and correct seasoning. Serve with chopped onions and thinly sliced black bread.

**Serves:** 4 to 6

# Steak Tartare and Caviar

*If you serve Steak Tartare with caviar, you can leave out the seasonings because caviar is all the seasoning you need. You don't have to buy Beluga or Sevruga, as whitefish roe seasons marvelously. Lumpfish roe, while fine for other dishes, will not do for this one, so be sure to read the label on all caviar jars carefully.*

**1 pound beef, cut into cubes (may be round, sirloin, or fillet, but must be absolutely fat-free)**
**8 ounces of black caviar (whitefish roe may be used)**
**1 onion, peeled and cut into quarters**
**Buttered toast halves, made from thinly cut white bread, crusts trimmed**

Place metal blade in food processor. Add meat to processor and grind. Pile ground meat into your loveliest bowl or dish. Set jar of caviar in a bowl filled with cracked ice and place beside ground meat. Place onion in food processor and chop finely. Spoon onion into a small dish and place beside meat and caviar. Wrap buttered toast in a white linen napkin and add to array surrounding the meat. Let guests help themselves to toast, which they will spread with meat and top with caviar and a sprinkling of onion. Serve with champagne or vodka.

**Serves:** 4 to 6

# Texas Tacos

**TACO SHELLS**

**1 cup all-purpose flour**
**⅓ cup cornmeal**
**½ teaspoon salt**
**2 tablespoons shortening**
**¼ to ½ cup warm water**

**TACO FILLING**

**1½ pounds beef, trimmed and cut into cubes**
**1 small onion, peeled**
**1 clove garlic, peeled**
**3 sprigs parsley**
**2 tablespoons oil**
**2 tablespoons chili powder**
**2 teaspoons ground cumin**
**½ teaspoon salt**
**¼ teaspoon celery seed**
**¼ teaspoon dried basil**
**1 six-ounce can tomato paste**
**1 cup water**

**TACO TOPPING**

**1 cup grated Cheddar cheese**
**1 cup shredded lettuce**
**½ cup chopped onion**
**1 tomato, diced**

*To make Taco Shells:*

Place metal blade in food processor. Add flour, cornmeal, salt, and shortening to processor. Process until shortening is cut into flour mixture. Add water and process until dough forms a ball. Cover and refrigerate for at least 1 hour. Form dough into 10 small balls. Roll out on a lightly floured board to 6-inch diameter.

Fry taco shells on a very lightly greased hot griddle or in a frying pan, for approximately 1 to 2 minutes on each side or until taco shells are dry and lightly browned. Fold each in half immediately upon removing from fry pan. You should have 10 taco shells.

**Yield:** 10 Taco shells

*To Make Taco Filling:*

Place metal blade in food processor. Add meat, onion, garlic, and parsley to processor and grind. You may have to do this in two or more steps, depending on the capacity of your processor. Heat oil in a large skillet and fry meat mixture until lightly browned. Add chili powder, cumin, salt, celery seed, basil, tomato paste, and water to skillet and simmer, stirring, for 15 minutes.

*Assembling Texas Tacos:*

Fill each taco shell with meat mixture and top with grated cheese, shredded lettuce, chopped onion, and diced tomato, which have been processed separately in food processor.

**Yield:** 10 tacos

# Lamb Kofta Kebabs

*The ground meat for Kofta Kebabs must be processed to a fine, pastelike consistency. Thanks to the food processor you can prepare this different—and inexpensive—dish without too much trouble. Serve Kofta Kebabs with a Rice Pilaff and with Raita Sauce* *(see page 78)**.*

**1 pound lean lamb, cubed**
**1 clove garlic, peeled**
**1 small onion, peeled and cut in half**
**1 egg**
**1 teaspoon ground cumin**
**1 tablespoon catsup**
**½ teaspoon curry powder**
**¼ teaspoon cinnamon**
**½ cup breadcrumbs**
**2 medium onions, peeled and quartered**

Place metal blade in food processor. Add lamb to processor and pulse on and off, scraping down sides of bowl, until meat is finely chopped. Add garlic, onion, egg, cumin, catsup, curry, and cinnamon to processor and pulse on and off, scraping down sides of bowl, for another 30 seconds. Add breadcrumbs and process until all ingredients are thoroughly blended and mixture has a pastelike consistency. Remove meat mixture from processor, and divide into 8 portions. Form meat mixture into thick, sausagelike patties around 4 kebab skewers. Each skewer should hold 2 kebabs and 2 onion quarters. Place skewers on a shallow broiling pan, and broil in a preheated 450-degree oven for 10 to 15 minutes, or until kebabs are brown and cooked.

**Serves:** 4

# Kibbeh Nayé

Kibbeh, *in all its variations, is a favorite dish throughout the Mideast. This recipe, made with raw lamb, may surprise many non-Mideasterners, who find themselves addicted to* kibbeh nayé *once they taste it.*

**1 pound lamb, cubed, trimmed, and absolutely fat-free (leg of lamb is best)**
**Salt and freshly ground black pepper to taste**
**1 large onion, peeled and cut into quarters**
**1 cup fine bulgur, or cracked wheat**
**Lemon quarters**
**Lettuce leaves**

Place metal blade in food processor. Add lamb, salt, pepper, and onion to processor and grind until meat is smooth and pastelike. Place bulgur in a strainer and rinse. Squeeze out water by hand and then add bulgur to meat mixture in processor. Process, pulsing on and off and scraping mixture down from sides of bowl until *kibbeh* is absolutely smooth. Spoon *kibbeh* onto lettuce leaves and serve with lemon quarters. You may also serve a bread basket of sesame crackers or pita bread along with the *kibbeh*.

**Serves:** 4 to 6

# Lamb-Stuffed Zucchini

**4 medium to large zucchini**
**1 pound lamb, trimmed and cut into cubes**
**1 medium onion, peeled and cut into quarters**
**¼ cup olive oil**
**1 cup cooked rice**
**Salt and freshly ground black pepper to taste**
**1 one-pound can stewed whole tomatoes, drained**
**2 teaspoons sugar, or more, to taste**
**¼ teaspoon hot paprika**
**⅛ teaspoon hot pepper flakes (optional)**

Peel zucchini and parboil until vegetable is barely tender, about 10 to 15 minutes. Remove zucchini from water and let cool. Place metal blade in food processor. Add lamb and onion to processor and grind. Heat oil in a large skillet and sauté meat-onion mixture until lightly brown. Stir in cooked rice and season with salt and pepper.

Cut cooled zucchini in half, scoop out centers, and discard. Fill zucchini halves with meat-rice mixture and place in baking dish. If there's any of the meat-rice mixture left, distribute it around the stuffed vegetables.

Place stewed tomatoes in processor and chop coarsely. Season to taste with sugar, paprika, and hot pepper flakes and pour over stuffed zucchini. Place baking dish in a preheated 350-degree oven and bake for 30 to 40 minutes.

**Serves:** 4 to 6

# Turkey Mousse San Francisco

**1 head iceberg lettuce**
**1 cup turkey or chicken broth**
**2 cups cooked turkey, cut into cubes**
**1 small onion, peeled**
**1 cup homemade Mayonnaise (see pages 60–61)**
**2 tablespoons lemon juice**
**¾ teaspoon salt**
**3 envelopes unflavored gelatin**
**½ cup water**
**1 cup whipped cream**
**2 cups whole cranberry sauce (optional)**

Place shredding disc in food processor. Core, rinse, and thoroughly drain lettuce. Shred enough lettuce to fill two tightly packed cups. Place metal blade in food processor. Return shredded lettuce to processor and add broth. Process until thoroughly blended. Add turkey, onion, mayonnaise, lemon juice, and salt. Process until completely smooth. Spoon turkey mixture into a bowl.

Mix gelatin and water. Heat, stirring, until gelatin is completely dissolved. Combine gelatin with turkey mixture. Chill until mixture mounds softly on a spoon.

Fold whipped cream into turkey mixture. Turn into a 6-cup mold and chill until firm. Unmold onto a serving platter and garnish with lettuce and cranberry sauce.

**Serves:** 8

*Turkey is low in calories, high in protein, and when it's not Thanksgiving, it's an especially good buy at most supermarkets. Here are two tasty recipes using turkey and pears. Both are easy to prepare, thanks to the food processor.*

# Turkey Burgers with Fruit Glaze

**1 pound of raw turkey meat, trimmed and cut into chunks**
**3 large ripe pears**
**1 small onion, peeled**
**Salt to taste**
**½ teaspoon poultry seasoning**
**¼ cup quick-cooking oats**
**1 egg**
**¼ to ½ cup all-purpose flour**
**¼ pound butter**
**1 cup cranberry juice cocktail**
**2 teaspoons cornstarch**
**2 teaspoons soy sauce**

Place metal blade in food processor. Add chunks of turkey to processor and grind. You should have about 2½ cups of ground meat. Peel, core, and halve one pear and add to turkey meat in food processor, along with onion, salt, poultry seasoning, oats, and egg. Blend thoroughly. Remove mixture from processor and form into 6 burgers. Roll burgers lightly in flour. Heat butter in a deep skillet and brown burgers on both sides. Cover skillet and continue cooking burgers over low heat for 30 to 40 minutes or until turkey is tender.

Before serving, beat together cranberry juice and cornstarch in a small bowl, making sure there are no lumps. Pour over burgers in skillet, mixing well with pan juices. Stir over low heat until glaze is bubbling and has thickened slightly.

Peel, core, and slice the two remaining pears and add to skillet. Stir in soy sauce. Allow glaze to simmer for two more minutes and serve.

**Serves:** 6

# Turkey 'n' Pear Chili

**½ pound raw turkey meat, cut into chunks**
**1 small onion, peeled**
**1 clove garlic, peeled**
**1 tablespoon oil**
**Salt and freshly ground black pepper to taste**
**1 teaspoon chili powder**
**1 teaspoon sugar**
**½ teaspoon mild paprika**
**Dash of cayenne pepper**
**1 one-pound can stewed tomatoes**
**1 teaspoon lemon juice**
**2 large Bartlett pears**
**1 teaspoon cornstarch**
**½ cup water**

Place metal blade in food processor. Add turkey, onion, and garlic clove to processor and grind. Heat oil in a large skillet. Add contents of processor to skillet and brown. Add seasonings to meat mixture and continue cooking for another 2 minutes. Place tomatoes in food processor and chop coarsely. Add tomatoes and lemon juice to mixture in skillet and simmer for 15 minutes, stirring occasionally.

Peel, halve, and core the two pears. Set aside. Blend cornstarch and water and stir into mixture in skillet. Bring to a boil and cook 1 more minute. Spoon meat mixture into pear halves and serve.

**Serves:** 4

# Chicken Apple Curry Sikander

**1 tablespoon curry powder**
**2 tablespoons butter**
**1 medium onion, peeled and cut in half**
**1 clove garlic, peeled**
**2 tablespoons all-purpose flour**
**2 cups chicken broth**
**2 McIntosh apples, peeled, cored, and cut in half**
**3 cups cooked chicken, cut into pieces**
**Salt and freshly ground black pepper to taste**

Sauté curry powder in butter in a large skillet over low heat for 2 to 3 minutes. Place metal blade in processor. Add onion and garlic to processor and chop. Add chopped onion, garlic, and flour to skillet and sauté, stirring until flour is lightly browned. Stir in broth and continue simmering until sauce thickens. Place apples and chicken in food processor and chop coarsely. Add chicken-apple mixture to sauce. Season to taste. Serve with cooked rice and such curry relishes as chutney, grated coconut, salted nuts, grated lemon rind, and pappadums.

**Serves:** 3 to 4

# Chicken Croquettes

**½ pound cooked chicken, cut into cubes**
**1 large boiled potato, peeled and cut into quarters**
**1 small onion, peeled and cut into 2 pieces**
**2 sprigs parsley**
**4 mushrooms**
**½ carrot, cleaned, scraped, and cut into 2 pieces**
**1 stalk celery, cut into 2 pieces**
**1 egg**
**4 slices white bread, crusts trimmed, cut into quarters**
**½ cup light cream**
**1 teaspoon salt**
**½ teaspoon white pepper**
**¼ cup all-purpose flour**
**½ cup homemade bread crumbs**
**Vegetable oil**

Place metal blade in food processor. Add chicken to processor and pulse on and off twice. Remove chicken from processor and reserve. Place all other ingredients, except for bread crumbs and oil, in processor and chop. Return ground chicken to processor and process, pulsing on and off and scraping down sides of bowl, until all ingredients are finely ground and thoroughly blended. Form chicken mixture into ovals and roll in bread crumbs. Heat oil in a large skillet and fry croquettes until golden brown. Serve with a cream sauce or a cheese sauce.

**Serves:** 4 to 6

# Chicken Timbale with Cheese Sauce

*Have a lot of leftover chicken? Turn it into a Timbale—the French answer to the American casserole.*

**CHICKEN TIMBALE**

**3 ounces Swiss cheese, cut into 3 pieces**
**1 pound cooked chicken, cut into chunks**
**¼ pound mushrooms**
**½ small onion, peeled**
**3 sprigs parsley**
**4 eggs**
**1 cup milk**
**Salt and freshly ground white pepper to taste**
**1 tablespoon grated Parmesan cheese**

**CHEESE SAUCE**

**4 ounces Cheddar cheese, cut into cubes**
**¼ pound butter, cut into pieces**
**¼ cup all-purpose flour**
**1 teaspoon salt**
**2 teaspoons dried chives**
**2 sprigs fresh dill**
**2 cups milk**

*To Make Chicken Timbale*

Place metal blade in food processor. Add cheese to processor and pulse on and off until cheese is finely diced. Remove cheese and reserve. Place chicken in food processor and pulse on and off until chicken is diced. Remove chicken and reserve. Add mushrooms, onion, and parsley to processor and chop coarsely.

Combine mixture with chicken and cheese, and spoon into a 1-quart ovenproof casserole, or a 3½- to 4-cup ring mold. Add eggs, milk, and seasonings to processor and process until thoroughly combined. Pour this mixture over chicken mixture. Sprinkle with Parmesan cheese.

Set casserole in a large baking dish and pour 2 inches of very hot water into the baking dish. Bake in a preheated 350-degree oven for 30 to 35 minutes or until a knife inserted 1 inch from center comes out clean. (While Timbale is baking make Cheese Sauce.) Remove Timbale from hot water. Gently loosen at top with spatula. Invert onto serving platter. Serve with Cheese Sauce.

*To Make Cheese Sauce:*

Place metal blade in food processor. Add cheese, butter, flour, salt, chives, and dill. Process until cheese is diced. Pour cheese mixture into a small saucepan. Add milk and cook over low heat until mixture comes to a boil and begins to thicken. Stir occasionally. You will have 2 cups of sauce.

**Serves:** 6

# Meat-Stuffed Crêpes Bolognese

**CRÊPES**

**¾ cups all-purpose flour**
**1 teaspoon salt**
**2 eggs**
**2 tablespoons melted butter**
**1¼ cup milk**

**MEAT FILLING**

**1 small onion, peeled and cut into quarters**
**2 stalks celery, cut into 1-inch pieces**
**1 small carrot, cleaned, scraped, and cut into 1-inch pieces**
**1 pound beef, cut into 1-inch cubes**
**3 tablespoons butter**
**3 tablespoons olive oil**
**Salt to taste**
**1 cup dry white wine**
**½ cup milk**
**1 eighteen-ounce can Italian-style plum tomatoes**

*To Make Crêpes:*

Place metal blade in food processor. Add flour, salt, eggs, and melted butter. With machine running, add milk through feed tube and process until batter has the consistency of light cream. Pour crêpe batter into a bowl and refrigerate for 2 hours.

*To Make Meat Filling:*

Place metal blade in food processor. Add onion and chop. Remove onion and reserve. Add celery and carrot to processor and process until finely chopped. Remove and reserve. Add meat to processor and process until ground. Remove and reserve.

Heat butter and oil in a large skillet. Sauté onions until they're translucent. Add celery and carrots, and cook an additional 3 minutes. Add ground meat to skillet and cook, breaking up lumps, until meat has lost its raw, red color. Season, and add wine to skillet. Cook, stirring, until wine has been absorbed. Add milk to skillet and continue cooking until milk has been absorbed.

Place metal blade in food processor. Add tomatoes to processor and chop coarsely. Spoon tomatoes into skillet, stir, and cover. Cook over a low flame for 1 to 1½ hours, stirring from time to time. Correct seasoning. While sauce is cooking, cook crêpes.

*To Cook Crêpes:*

Lightly butter one or two 6-inch Teflon or stick-proof skillets. Using a small ladle or a 2 tablespoon measuring cup, pour enough batter into pan to coat the bottom. Tilt the pan and cook crêpes over medium-high heat until lightly browned. Slide crêpe out of pan onto plate and allow crêpes to cool before filling. Fill crêpes with 2 to 3 tablespoons of Meat Filling. Fold crêpes in half. Spoon a small amount of Meat Filling on the bottom of a baking dish and place folded, filled crêpes on top. Pour any remaining Meat Filling over crêpes. Bake in a preheated 350-degree oven for 20 to 25 minutes or until crêpes and filling are hot.

**Serves:** 6 (2 crêpes per person)

# FISH AND SHELLFISH

The most complicated fish dish can grace your table this evening, thanks to the food processor. Fish quenelles, those delicate dumplings made from a forcemeat of fish, are now easy to prepare. No need to press fish through a fine sieve or work away with a mortar and pestle. Your food processor will do all the work in seconds. And this is just one of the ways you can use the food processor in the preparation of fish and shellfish.

You will find a variety of fish dishes in this chapter. Some, such as Cold Salmon Mousse, will provide an epicurean delight for your next dinner party. Others, such as New England Fish Hash, make tasty use of leftovers for a simple family meal. With your food processor you can soon become an expert at preparing a myriad of wonderful fish and shellfish dishes.

# Fried Clam Fritters

**1 pint fresh clams, out of the shell,**
**cleaned, and drained**
**2 eggs**
**⅓ cup milk**
**1 cup all-purpose flour**
**2 teaspoons baking powder**
**Salt and freshly ground black pepper to taste**
**2 cups oil**

Place metal blade in food processor. Add clams to processor and chop coarsely. Add all other ingredients, except oil, to processor and pulse on and off, scraping down sides of bowl, until all ingredients are thoroughly combined.

Heat oil in a large skillet and drop tablespoonfuls of fritter mixture into hot oil. Fry until fritters are brown on both sides, about 3 to 5 minutes. Remove with slotted spoon and drain on paper towels. Serve with tartar sauce and a large tossed salad.

**Serves:** 6

# Spicy Creole Crab Cakes

**1 pound cooked crab meat, picked over to remove all bits of cartilage**
**¼ small onion, peeled**
**1 egg**
**1 cup homemade bread crumbs**
**1 teaspoon dry mustard**
**Dash of cayenne pepper**
**¼ cup, or more, milk**
**4 tablespoons all-purpose flour**
**¼ pound butter**

Place metal blade in food processor. Add crab meat to processor and grind. Add all remaining ingredients, except for flour and butter, and pulse on and off, scraping down sides of bowl, until crab meat mixture is thoroughly blended. Form crab meat mixture into flat cakes. Roll lightly in flour. Heat butter in a large skillet and fry crab cakes until they are brown on both sides.

**Serves:** 4

# Gefilte Fish (Fish Balls)

**GEFILTE FISH**

**3 pounds filleted fish (may be carp, whitefish, or a combination of both) cut into chunks**
**3 medium onions, peeled and cut into quarters**
**2 eggs**
**1 teaspoon salt**
**½ teaspoon white pepper**
**½ cup homemade bread crumbs or ½ cup matzo meal**

**STOCK**

**1 onion, peeled and cut in half**
**3 carrots, cleaned and scraped**
**5 sprigs parsley**
**Heads, skin, and bones of fish**
**Salt and freshly ground pepper**
**Water**

*To Make Gefilte Fish:*

Place metal blade in food processor. Add filleted fish chunks to food processor and grind. Add quartered onions, eggs, salt, pepper, and bread crumbs or matzo meal and continue processing until very smooth. The processing may have to be done in two or more steps, depending on the capacity of your processor. Remove mixture to a large bowl. Form fish mixture into small balls.

*To Make Stock:*

Slice onion and carrots and place in a large saucepan. Add parsley; heads, skin, and bones of fish; and salt and freshly ground pepper. Cover with at least 1 quart of water and bring stock to a boil. Simmer for 15 minutes.

Add fish balls. Add water, if necessary, to cover. Keep stock at a simmer, cover pot, and cook 2 hours. Remove gefilte fish balls from stock. Strain stock and pour around fish balls. Serve when chilled.

**Serves:** 6 to 8

# Magda's Fish Salad

**1 onion, peeled and cut in half**
**3 stalks celery, leaves and all, cut in half**
**2 tablespoons vinegar**
**⅛ teaspoon red pepper flakes**
**2 carrots, cleaned, scraped, and cut in half**
**Salt and freshly ground black pepper to taste**
**4 pounds halibut fillets**
**2 stalks celery, each cut into 3 pieces**
**2 green peppers, each seeded, cored, and cut into 3 or 4 pieces**
**2 cups homemade Mayonnaise (see pages 60–61)**
**Salt and freshly ground black pepper to taste**

Place first 6 ingredients in a large pot or fish poacher with 2 quarts of water. Bring water to a boil and continue boiling for 20 minutes. Reduce heat until water simmers, and slip halibut fillets into this *court bouillon*. Poach until fork pierces the fish easily. Depending on the thickness of the fillets, this can take anywhere from 10 to 20 minutes. Remove fish from bouillon and allow to cool.

Place metal blade in food processor. Cut fish into large pieces and place in processor. Chop coarsely. You may have to do this in two or more steps, depending on the capacity of your processor. Remove fish to a large bowl. Place celery and green peppers in processor and chop coarsely. Add to fish, along with mayonnaise and seasonings. Stir to combine and pile into your prettiest glass bowl. Chill at least 4 hours before serving.

**Serves:** 8

# New England Fish Hash

**1 pound cooked fillet of cod or halibut, cut into chunks**
**4 potatoes, peeled, cubed, boiled, and drained**
**1 small onion, peeled**
**Salt and freshly ground black pepper to taste**
**¼ pound salt pork, cut into cubes**

Place metal blade in food processor. Add fish chunks to processor and chop coarsely. Add potatoes, onions, salt, and pepper to processor. Scrape down sides of bowl and process until all ingredients are thoroughly combined.

Render salt pork in a large skillet. Remove scraps and leave fat in pan. Spoon fish mixture from processor into skillet and stir until thoroughly heated. Continue cooking until mixture is well browned. Fold hash as you would an omelet and serve.

**Serves:** 4

# Quenelles de Poisson et Sauce aux Crevettes et Vin

**QUENELLES DE POISSON**

**1 pound fillet of flounder, sole, or salmon, cut into chunks**
**1 cup water**
**4 tablespoons butter**
**¼ teaspoon salt**
**½ cup all-purpose flour**
**2 eggs**
**3 sprigs parsley**
**4 mushrooms**
**1 small onion, peeled**
**3 tablespoons heavy sweet cream**

**SAUCE AUX CREVETTES ET VIN**

**½ pound shrimp, cooked, cleaned, and deveined, each shrimp cut in half**
**3 tablespoons butter**
**3 scallions, each one cut into 3 pieces**
**3 tablespoons all-purpose flour**
**2 cups dry white wine**
**2 tablespoons tomato paste**
**½ cup tomato sauce**
**4 sprigs parsley**
**Salt and freshly ground black pepper to taste**
**1 cup heavy sweet cream**

*To Make Sauce:*

Place metal blade in food processor. Add cooked shrimp to processor and chop coarsely. Heat butter in a saucepan. Add scallions and flour and cook for 2 minutes, stirring. Add wine, tomato paste, tomato sauce, parsley, and salt and pepper. Bring to a simmer and cook for 30 minutes. Pour sauce into processor, scrape down bowl, and process shrimp and sauce for about 20 seconds. Return contents of processor to saucepan and stir in cream. Bring to a simmer and cook for 3 to 5 minutes. Correct seasoning and serve over quenelles.

**Serves:** 8

*To Make Quenelles:*

Place metal blade in food processor. Add fish to processor and grind until smooth. Remove and reserve ground fish.

Combine water and butter in a small saucepan and bring to a boil. Quickly stir in salt and all the flour. Stir with a wooden spoon and cook over low heat for approximately 2 minutes or until mixture coats the bottom of the saucepan and begins to move away from the sides of the saucepan. Place this flour-butter mixture in food processor and process until smooth. Add all remaining ingredients and process for another 20 seconds or so, until everything is well blended. Return reserved ground fish to processor. Scrape down sides of bowl and continue processing, pulsing on and off, until all ingredients are a smooth blend. Depending on the size of your processor bowl, you may have to do this in two steps.

Bring 2 to 3 inches of salted water to a slow simmer in a 12-inch skillet. Carefully slip tablespoonsful of quenelle batter into simmering water and poach for 15 to 20 minutes uncovered. Do not allow water to boil. Quenelles are done when they have approximately doubled in size. Remove quenelles with a slotted spoon and place in a buttered casserole. Serve with hot Sauce aux Crevettes et Vin.

# Salmon Steak with Lettuce Sauce

**1 head, or more, iceberg lettuce**
**½ small onion, peeled**
**1 cup sour cream**
**2 tablespoons lime or lemon juice**
**1½ teaspoons salt**
**¼ teaspoon white pepper**
**1 cup milk**
**¼ pound butter**
**1 medium potato, peeled, cubed, boiled, and drained**
**6 salmon steaks**
**Salt and pepper to taste**
**½ cup dry vermouth**
**6 lemon slices**
**6 tablespoons red caviar (salmon roe)**
**Ripe black olives**

Place metal blade in food processor. Core, rinse, and drain lettuce. Chop lettuce in food processor until you have 4 tightly packed cups of chopped lettuce. Remove and reserve. Chop onion in processor. Add sour cream, lime or lemon juice, salt, and pepper and blend. Gradually add chopped lettuce until you have a smooth sauce. When sauce is thoroughly blended, remove to a bowl and reserve.

Heat milk and 4 tablespoons butter in a saucepan. Place cooked potato in processor. With machine on, gradually add milk-butter mixture to potato. Scrape down sides of bowl and pulse on and off. Potato should be smooth, but do not overprocess, or potato will have a pastelike consistency. Allow potato mixture to cool, then blend gradually into reserved lettuce sauce, combining with a spoon and not the processor.

Sprinkle salmon steaks with salt and pepper and place in a baking pan. Cut remaining butter into 6 pieces and place a piece of butter on each salmon steak. Pour vermouth over fish. Cover pan with foil and bake in a prehcated 400-degree oven for about 20 minutes or until fish flakes easily with a fork.

Chill salmon steaks. Serve with a dollop of Lettuce Sauce on top and lemon slices. Garnish with red caviar and black olives.

**Serves:** 6

# Cold Salmon Mousse

**3 tablespoons lemon juice**
**2 tablespoons cold water**
**2 envelopes unflavored gelatin**
**⅔ cup boiling water**
**2 stalks celery, each one cut into 3 pieces**
**1 small onion, peeled and cut into 2 pieces**
**¼ medium cucumber, peeled and cut into 4 pieces**
**½ carrot, cleaned, scraped, and cut into 2 pieces**
**2 sprigs parsley**
**½ cup homemade Mayonnaise (see pages 60–61)**
**1 cup heavy sweet cream**
**¼ teaspoon white pepper**
**1 teaspoon salt**
**3 sprigs fresh dill**
**1 pound fresh salmon steaks, poached, with skin and bones removed and cut into pieces (or 2 seven-and-three-quarter-ounce cans salmon, drained)**

Place metal blade in food processor. Place lemon juice and cold water in food processor. Sprinkle gelatin on top and let stand 1 minute. Add boiling water and blend for about 10 seconds. Add celery, onion, cucumber, carrot, parsley, and mayonnaise to processor. Pulse once or twice, until vegetables are coarsely chopped. Scrape down sides of bowl, add cream, pepper, salt, and dill, and pulse on and off once again. Add salmon to processor, scrape down sides of bowl, and process, pulsing on and off until mousse mixture is thoroughly smooth. Depending on size of your processor bowl, you may have to do this in two steps. Spoon mousse into a 5-cup fish-shaped mold. Chill overnight or until firm. Serve on a bed of chopped salad greens and garnish with lemon slices and pimientos.

**Serves:** 6

# Oysters New Orleans

**3 scallions, each cut into 3 pieces**
**1 stalk celery, cut into 3 pieces**
**2 stalks fresh fennel or finocchio, each stalk cut into 3 pieces**
**4 sprigs Italian parsley**
**4 tablespoons butter**
**2 cups watercress**
**¼ pound butter, cut into 6 or 8 pieces**
**½ cup homemade bread crumbs**
**½ cup anisette liqueur**
**Salt and freshly ground black pepper to taste**
**Few grains cayenne pepper**
**2 dozen absolutely fresh oysters, on the half-shell**

Place metal blade in food processor. Add scallions, celery, fennel, and parsley to processor and chop coarsely. Melt 4 tablespoons of butter in a large skillet and add mixture from food processor. Sauté until vegetables are limp, about 3 to 5 minutes. Add watercress and cook, stirring, until watercress has wilted.

Return ingredients from skillet to processor and add ¼ pound butter, bread crumbs, and anisette. Process until mixture is thoroughly blended and smooth. Season to taste.

Place approximately 1 tablespoonful of mixture on top of each oyster and bake oysters in a preheated 450-degree oven until topping and oysters are hot, approximately 4 to 5 minutes.

**Serves:** 4

# Sole Mousse and Cucumber Sauce

**SOLE MOUSSE**

**1¼ pounds cooked fillet of sole***
**1 cup milk**
**1 small onion, peeled**
**2 tablespoons all-purpose flour**
**6 eggs**
**3 sprigs parsley**
**½ teaspoon salt**
**3 sprigs fresh dill**

**CUCUMBER SAUCE**

**½ cucumber, peeled and cut into 3 pieces**
**½ small onion, peeled**
**4 sprigs fresh dill**
**1 teaspoon salt**
**¼ teaspoon white pepper**
**2 cups sour cream**

*To Make Sole Mousse:*

Place metal blade in food processor. Add fish to processor and grind until smooth. Scrape down sides of bowl and add all other ingredients, pulsing on and off until mixture is smooth and thoroughly combined. Spoon mousse mixture into a well-greased 6-cup ring mold. Bake in a preheated 400-degree oven for about 50 to 60 minutes or until top is brown and puffy and knife inserted in center comes out clean. Remove from oven and serve warm with Cucumber Sauce.

*Cooked or canned salmon, tuna, or flounder, or cooked, cleaned, and deveined shrimp may be substituted for the sole.

*To Make Cucumber Sauce:*

Place metal blade in food processor. Add cucumber, onion, and dill to processor and chop coarsely. Add salt, pepper, and sour cream and blend thoroughly.

Spoon Cucumber Sauce into a bowl and serve with Sole Mousse.

**Serves:** 8

# Tuna Shrimp Pie

**1 single nine-inch baked pie crust shell (see page 204 All-American Piecrust Dough)**
**1 seven-ounce can tuna, drained**
**½ pound shrimp, cooked, shelled, and deveined, each shrimp cut in half**
**½ cup pimiento-stuffed small green olives**
**½ cup heavy sweet cream**
**2 cups Béchamel sauce (see page 139)**
**Salt and freshly ground black pepper to taste**
**½ teaspoon mild paprika**
**Few grains cayenne pepper**

Place baked pie shell in oven and keep warm, at approximately 200 degrees, until ready to use.

Place metal blade in food processor. Add tuna and shrimp to processor and chop, pulsing on and off and scraping down sides of bowl. Ingredients should be coarsely chopped and combined. Stir ¼ cup of olives into tuna-shrimp mixture, combining with a spoon. Reserve remainder of the olives for garnish. Place mixture in a large skillet or saucepan and add cream, Béchamel Sauce, and seasonings and bring to a simmer over low heat, stirring from time to time. Pour mixture into pie shell, garnish with remaining olives, and serve at once.

**Serves:** 6

# Béchamel Sauce

**4 tablespoons butter**
**4 tablespoons all-purpose flour**
**2 cups light sweet cream**
**Salt and freshly ground white pepper to taste**
**⅛ teaspoon nutmeg (optional)**

Melt butter in a saucepan. Add flour and cook over low heat, stirring, for 3 to 5 minutes, making sure that flour does not burn. Bring cream to a simmer and add cream to butter-flour mixture. Whisk mixture, allowing it to come to a simmer, and cook, whisking or stirring for 3 to 5 minutes, until mixture thickens. Season to taste.

**Yield:** Approximately 2 cups

# Tuna Timbale

**2 cans (approximately 7 ounces each) tuna, drained**
**½ cup homemade bread crumbs**
**4 tablespoons butter, cut into 4 pieces**
**2 eggs**
**3 sprigs parsley**
**3 tablespoons heavy sweet cream**
**Salt and freshly ground white pepper to taste**
**Dash of cayenne pepper**

Place metal blade in food processor. Add tuna to processor and chop. Add other ingredients, one at a time, and continue processing, scraping down sides of bowl, until mixture is well blended. Spoon mixture into a buttered 4-cup mold or loaf pan. Place mold or pan into a larger pan of hot water and bake in a preheated 375-degree oven for 30 minutes.

**Serves:** 4 to 6

# Seafood Crêpes with Cheese Sauce

**CRÊPES**

**¾ cup all-purpose flour**
**1 teaspoon salt**
**2 eggs**
**2 tablespoons melted butter**
**1¼ cups milk**

**CHEESE SAUCE**

**4 ounces Cheddar cheese, cut in cubes**
**¼ pound butter, cut into pieces**
**¼ cup all-purpose flour**
**1 teaspoon salt**
**2 teaspoons dried chives**
**1 sprig fresh dill**
**2 cups milk**

**SEAFOOD FILLING**

**½ small onion, peeled**
**¼ pound mushrooms, cut into quarters**
**1 pound combination of mixed seafood: crab, shrimp, cod, or flounder**
**1 cup Cheese Sauce (above)**
**1 teaspoon salt**
**½ teaspoon pepper**

*To Make Crêpes Batter:*

Place metal blade in food processor. Add flour, salt, eggs, and melted butter. With machine on, add milk through feed tube and process until batter has the consistency of light cream. Pour crêpe batter into a bowl and refrigerate for 2 hours.

*To Make Cheese Sauce:*

Place metal blade in food processor. Add cheese, butter, flour, salt, chives, and dill. Process until cheese is chopped. Pour cheese mixture into a small saucepan. Add milk and cook over low heat until mixture comes to a boil and begins to thicken. Stir occasionally. You should have two cups of Cheese Sauce. Reserve.

*To Make Filling:*

Place metal blade in food processor. Add onion and mushrooms and process 10 seconds or until chopped. Add seafood. Process 10 seconds or until ground. Add all but 2 tablespoons of the cheese sauce, salt, and pepper and process 5 seconds. You should have 3 cups.

*To Cook Crêpes:*

Lightly grease one or two 6-inch teflon or nonstick skillets. Using a small ladle or a 2-tablespoon measuring cup, pour enough batter into pan to coat the bottom. Tilt the pan so batter thoroughly covers pan bottom. Cook each crêpe until lightly browned and then slide out of pan onto a flat plate. Allow crêpes to cool. Fill with ¼ cup seafood mixture and roll.

**Yield:** 12 crêpes

*To Assemble Crêpes:*

Spread a small amount of remaining cheese sauce on the bottom of a 13×9×3-inch baking dish. Place crêpes seam side down in pan. Top with remaining cheese sauce. Bake in preheated 350-degree oven for 20 to 25 minutes or until sauce is bubbling and beginning to brown on edges.

**Serves:** 4

# VEGETABLES, SALADS, AND STUFFINGS

Vegetables have been the object of bad publicity over the years. From childhood on, we are told how good vegetables are *for* us, but not how good they *are*. Nutrition rather than flavor is emphasized until vegetables soon have about as much appeal as medicine. Too often children grow up to despise vegetables, never really having had an opportunity to taste and appreciate them. With the advent of the food processor, the time has come to reverse all the antivegetable propaganda. Properly prepared, vegetables are delicious, nutritious, and beautiful. With the aid of a food processor you can turn the most ordinary vegetables into delicately spiced and flavored purees, just like the vegetable purees served at the most expensive French restaurants. In addition, your processor will shred cabbage for cole slaw, puree avocado for perfect guacamole, and grate potatoes for potato pancakes—all in a matter of seconds.

# Artichokes Stuffed with Ham and Mushrooms

**4 large artichokes**
**¼ pound boiled ham, cut into cubes or strips**
**¼ pound mushrooms**
**1 small onion, peeled**
**½ cup olive oil**
**½ cup homemade bread crumbs**
**1 cup dry white wine**
**1 cup chicken broth**

Cut off the stems of the artichokes and the tips of the leaves and remove tough outer leaves. Open up center of each artichoke and, using a spoon or a melon ball cutter, remove and discard choke from center of each artichoke. Wash artichokes well and reserve.

Place metal blade in food processor. Chop ham, mushrooms, and onion in processor. Heat olive oil in a large skillet and sauté ingredients from food processor for 10 to 15 minutes. Remove from heat and stir bread crumbs into mixture in skillet. Combine thoroughly. Stuff artichokes with mixture. Place artichokes in a baking dish, and pour wine and chicken broth over them. Cover dish with foil and place in a preheated 350-degree oven for 1 hour or until artichokes are tender. Test by removing an artichoke leaf and tasting for tenderness.

**Serves:** 4

# Glazed Carrots

**1½ pounds carrots, cleaned and scraped**
**1 cup beef bouillon or 1 cup water**
**1 tablespoon sugar, or more, to taste**
**Salt and freshly ground black pepper to taste**
**¼ pound butter**

Place slicing disc in food processor. Slice carrots and place them in a saucepan. Add all other ingredients and cook until carrots are tender and the liquid has become a glaze. The length of cooking time will depend on the age of the carrots and can range anywhere from 15 to 40 minutes. Carrots should be firm to tender, and not mushy.

**Serves:** 4 to 6

# A Bouquet of Cole Slaws

*Cole slaws are a marvelous accompaniment to seafood, sandwiches, fried chicken, and barbecues. The food processor will slice or shred cabbage for a variety of slaws. Here are several recipes from which you can easily adapt your own favorites.*

# Cabbage and Bean Slaw

**½ head of cabbage (about 1 pound), cored and cut into wedges**
**2 carrots, cleaned and scraped**
**2 stalks celery**
**1 small onion, peeled**
**1 sixteen-ounce can red kidney beans, drained**
**½ teaspoon salt**
**1 cup homemade Mayonnaise (see pages 60–61)**
**1 tablespoon wine vinegar**
**3 tablespoons olive oil**

Place slicing disc in food processor. Slice cabbage, carrots, celery, and onion, doing this in as many steps as necessary until all vegetables are sliced. Place vegetables in a large bowl and add drained beans.Sprinkle salt on vegetables and toss with mayonnaise. Combine vinegar and olive oil and pour over slaw. Toss again until all ingredients are combined.

**Serves:** 4 to 6

# Gingery Fruit Slaw

**½ head of cabbage (about 1 pound), cored and cut into wedges**
**2 Bartlett pears, halved and cored**
**⅓ cup seedless grapes**
**1 cup homemade Mayonnaise (see pages 60–61)**
**3 teaspoons grated lemon rind**
**2 tablespoons lemon juice**
**2 teaspoons sugar**
**½ teaspoon ground ginger**
**¼ teaspoon salt**

Place slicing disc in food processor. Slice cabbage, doing this in as many steps as necessary. Remove cabbage to a large salad bowl. Place metal blade in processor and coarsely chop pears. Remove to salad bowl and add whole grapes to salad bowl. Using metal blade, blend remaining ingredients in food processor. Pour mixture over ingredients in bowl and toss. Chill 30 minutes before serving.

**Serves:** 4 to 6

# Hot Cole Slaw with Sherry Wine and Cheese

**½ head of cabbage (about 1 pound), cored and cut into wedges**
**2 small onions, peeled**
**1 medium carrot, cleaned, scraped, and cut into 3 pieces**
**2 tablespoons butter**
**1 tablespoon sugar**
**½ teaspoon salt**
**¼ cup dry sherry**
**¼ cup Parmesan cheese, grated**

Place slicing disc in food processor and slice cabbage, doing this in as many steps as necessary until all cabbage is sliced. Slice onion in food processor. Remove cabbage and onion and reserve. Change to metal blade and chop carrot fine in food processor.

Melt butter in a large skillet and sauté all vegetables for 5 minutes. Add seasonings and sherry to skillet and continue cooking for 10 minutes, stirring from time to time. Place mixture in a baking dish, sprinkle with Parmesan cheese, and place in a preheated 425-degree oven until cheese melts, approximately 10 minutes.

**Serves:** 4 to 6

# Old-Fashioned Cole Slaw

**1 small head of cabbage (about 1½ to 2 pounds), cored and cut into wedges**
**2 carrots, cleaned, scraped, and cut in half**
**1 green pepper, cored, seeded, and cut into 4 pieces**
**1 small onion, peeled**
**1 cup homemade Mayonnaise (see pages 60–61)**
**2 tablespoons vinegar**
**¼ cup milk**
**Salt and freshly ground black pepper to taste**
**2 teaspoons sugar**

Place slicing disc in food processor. Slice cabbage, doing this in as many steps as necessary until all cabbage is sliced. Remove cabbage to a large bowl. Slice carrots and add to cabbage. Change to metal blade and chop green pepper and onion in food processor; add to cabbage and carrots. Blend all other ingredients in food processor, using metal blade, and pour dressing over vegetables. Toss to combine thoroughly, and serve.

**Serves:** 6 to 8

# Cabbage and Bow-Tie Noodles

**½ head of cabbage (about 1 pound), cored and cut into wedges**
**Salt**
**1 large onion, peeled and cut into 4 pieces**
**1 cup cooking oil**
**2 tablespoons sugar, or more, to taste**
**Salt and freshly ground black pepper to taste**
**½ pound of bow-tie noodles, cooked *al dente*, or slightly firm**

Place slicing disc in food processor. Slice cabbage. Remove to a large bowl and salt liberally. Allow cabbage to stand for half an hour and then, taking handfuls of cabbage, squeeze out excess water. Reserve cabbage.

Place metal blade in food processor and chop onion. Heat ¼ of oil in a large skillet and sauté onions until translucent. Add cabbage to skillet and sauté, stirring from time to time and adding more oil as necessary. Cover skillet and cook over low heat for about 30 minutes or until cabbage is completely tender. Add sugar, salt, and lots of black pepper. Cabbage should have a sweet, spicy flavor. Cook an additional 5 minutes and then stir in cooked noodles. Correct seasoning and serve piping hot. This dish is especially good with roast duck or roast goose.

**Serves:** 8

# Cucumber and Onion Salad

**4 large cucumbers, peeled**
**2 large onions, peeled**
**Salt**
**3 cups water**
**4 tablespoons sugar, or more, to taste**
**1 cup white vinegar**
**Paprika**

Place slicing disc in food processor. Slice cucumbers and onions and remove to a large bowl. Sprinkle cucumbers and onions liberally with salt and stir. Allow vegetables to remain in salt for 20 minutes or until wilted. Squeeze water out of vegetables and return to bowl. (If you prefer a crisper salad, you may omit salting step.)

Combine all other ingredients and correct seasoning to taste. Pour water-vinegar mixture over cucumbers and onions and chill. Allow to stand at least 4 hours before serving.

This salad will be fine the next day, the day after, or as long as it lasts.

**Serves:** 8 to 10

# Jellied Mousse of Cucumber

**2 cucumbers, peeled and quartered**
**1 envelope unflavored gelatin**
**¼ cup cold water**
**2 tablespoons boiling water**
**1 tablespoon lemon juice**
**½ cup homemade Mayonnaise (see pages 60–61)**
**1 teaspoon salt**
**¼ teaspoon freshly ground white pepper**
**1 cup heavy whipping cream**

Place metal blade in food processor. Add cucumbers to processor and puree, scraping down sides of bowl.

Place gelatin in a small bowl and soften in cold water. Add boiling water and stir. Add gelatin mixture and remaining ingredients to food processor and process until mixture is thoroughly smooth and blended. Pour mixture into a 1-quart mold and chill overnight.

**Serves:** 8

# Fiesta Three-Bean Salad

**1 green pepper, cored, seeded, and cut into 4 pieces**
**1 large onion, peeled**
**1 clove garlic, peeled**
**1 sixteen-ounce can chick peas, drained**
**1 sixteen-ounce can red kidney beans, drained**
**1 sixteen-ounce can cut green beans, drained**
**2 tablespoons olive oil**
**5 tablespoons cider vinegar**
**¼ cup dark molasses**
**1½ teaspoons salt**
**Freshly ground black pepper to taste**
**1 teaspoon Worcestershire sauce**
**¼ teaspoon Tabasco**
**1½ teaspoons chili powder**
**½ teaspoon dry mustard**

Place metal blade in food processor. Chop green pepper, onion, and garlic clove in food processor. Remove to a large salad bowl. Add all beans to salad bowl. Place all other ingredients in food processor and blend thoroughly. Pour over salad ingredients and toss well. Chill two or more hours before serving, stirring occasionally.

**Serves:** 6

# Guacamole Salad

**2 large ripe avocados, peeled, pitted, and cut into chunks**
**1 clove garlic, peeled**
**1 small onion, peeled**
**2 teaspoons lemon juice**
**¼ teaspoon Tabasco, or a Mexican hot chili pepper, fresh or canned**
**1 tomato, cut in half**
**½ cup mayonnaise**
**Salt to taste**

Place metal blade in food processor. Add all ingredients, except mayonnaise and salt, to processor and chop coarsely, pulsing on and off and scraping down sides of bowl. Add mayonnaise and salt and blend. Serve on lettuce, as a salad, or with corn chips or warm tortillas, as a dip.

**Serves:** 6

# Gallatin's Spiced Stuffed Tomatoes

*Gallatin's Restaurant, in Monterey, California, is deservedly proud of its varied menu, which features such items as Abalone Puffs, as well as more familiar continental dishes. The following is one of their more original dishes.*

**LETTUCE FILLING FOR BAKED TOMATOES**

**2 heads iceberg lettuce, broken into large wedges**
**2 scallions, cut into 2 pieces each**
**3 tablespoons butter**
**Pinch of cayenne pepper**
**Pinch of nutmeg**
**Salt to taste**

## BAKED TOMATOES

**6 ripe medium tomatoes**
**¼ pound Gruyère cheese, cut into cubes**
**¼ cup sugar**
**¼ cup butter**
**Pinch of salt**

*To Make Lettuce Filling:*

Place metal blade in food processor. Chop lettuce and scallions in processor. You should have 8 cups of tightly-packed shredded lettuce. Steam lettuce and scallions in very little water until tender. Drain and cool. Using metal blade, puree lettuce mixture in processor.

Melt butter in a saucepan. Add lettuce and remaining ingredients. Cook, stirring, until most of the liquid is evaporated, about 10 minutes. Use as a filling for Baked Tomatoes.

*To Make Baked Tomatoes:*

Cut tops from tomatoes and scoop out insides. Place metal blade in food processor. Add tomato pulp to processor and chop. Reserve. Spoon Lettuce Filling into tomato cases. Place Gruyère cheese cubes in food processor and chop; sprinkle filled tomatoes with the cheese.

Place tomato pulp in a saucepan and add sugar, butter, and salt. Cook tomato mixture until it is soft and well blended. Pour tomato mixture into a buttered baking dish. Arrange stuffed tomatoes on top, and bake in a preheated 400-degree oven for 15 minutes.

**Serves:** 6

# A Wealth of Vegetable Purees

*The French have long served vegetable purees with meat and fish dishes. Pureed vegetables are delicious, can be prepared in advance, and are a favorite in many restaurants that specialize in the* nouvelle cuisine*—the new and interesting approach to cooking. Whereas* nouvelle cuisine *in the United States has come to mean lower calories, French* nouvelle cuisine *concentrates on many courses of small amounts of very rich food, beautifully presented. Vegetable purees are an important part of this latest fashion in food, because the bright orange of a carrot puree or the deep green of a broccoli puree is beautiful as well as delicious.*

# Puree of Carrots with Cream

**2 pounds carrots, cleaned, scraped, cut in pieces, and cooked**
**6 tablespoons butter, softened**
**½ cup heavy sweet cream**
**Salt and freshly ground white pepper to taste**

Place metal blade in food processor. Place carrots and butter in processor and puree, pulsing on and off, scraping down sides of bowl when necessary. Do not overprocess. Carrot puree should not be as fine as baby food. Add cream and seasoning and process only until all ingredients are thoroughly blended. Heat before serving.

**Serves:** 4

# Puree of Broccoli

**1 bunch broccoli, cooked**
**¼ pound butter, softened and cut into 4 pieces**
**Salt and freshly ground black pepper to taste**

Placc metal blade in food processor. Cut broccoli into large pieces and place in processor. Add all other ingredients, and puree, pulsing on and off, scraping down sides of bowl. Do not overprocess. Broccoli puree should not be as fine as baby food. Heat before serving.

**Serves:** 4

# Quick White Bean Puree

**1 sixteen-ounce can white cannellini beans**
**1 clove garlic, peeled**
**4 tablespoons butter**
**Salt and freshly ground white pepper**

Pour cannellini beans into a colander. Drain off all can juices and rinse. Drain again. Place metal blade in food processor. Add cannellini beans to processor and, with machine on, drop garlic through feed tube into processor. Pulse on and off, scraping down sides of bowl until beans are pureed. Heat butter in a saucepan and add pureed beans to saucepan. Season to taste and heat before serving.

**Serves:** 4

# Green Beans and Almond Puree

**1½ pounds green beans, cooked and drained**
**1 cup chicken broth**
**¼ pound butter**
**½ cup sour cream**
**Salt and freshly ground black pepper to taste**
**¼ cup slivered almonds**

Place metal blade in food processor. Add green beans and chicken broth to processor. Puree, pulsing on and off, scraping down sides of bowl. Do not overprocess. Green bean puree should not be as fine as baby food.

Melt butter in a skillet and spoon mixture from processor into skillet. Cook, stirring, over low heat, until puree begins to simmer; then stir in sour cream and season to taste. Continue cooking until puree is thoroughly hot. Serve with slivered almonds as a garnish.

**Serves:** 6

# Potato and Celery Root Puree

**2 large celery roots (celery knob), peeled, cubed, cooked, and drained**
**4 large potatoes, peeled, cubed, cooked, and drained**
**1 cup chicken broth**
**Salt and freshly ground black pepper to taste**
**¼ pound sweet butter, cut into 6 to 8 pieces**
**½ cup, or more, heavy sweet cream**

Place metal blade in food processor. Add cooked celery root to processor and start to puree, pulsing on and off. Add potatoes and pulse on and off once again. Scrape down sides of bowl and add all other ingredients. Do not overprocess, or potatoes will have a pastelike consistency. Process only until mixture is smooth and ingredients are combined. Heat before serving.

**Serves:** 6 to 8

# White Bean and Chestnut Puree

**3 cups cooked and drained white beans (may be canned)**
**1 cup canned unsweetened chestnut puree**
**Salt and freshly ground black pepper to taste**
**¼ pound butter**
**½ cup heavy sweet cream**
**1 teaspoon sugar, or more, to taste**

Place metal blade in food processor. Add beans to processor and puree until completely smooth. Add chestnut puree to processor and continue processing until completely blended. Season. Melt butter in a saucepan and add bean-chestnut mixture. Cook, stirring, for 2 to 3 minutes and then stir in cream gradually. Add sugar to taste and continue stirring over low heat until puree is thoroughly warm. This puree is especially delicious with roast lamb.

**Serves:** 6 to 8

# Creamy Spinach Puree

**2 pounds cooked spinach**
**¼ pound butter**
**1 tablespoon all-purpose flour**
**Salt and freshly ground black pepper to taste**
**Pinch of nutmeg**
**1 cup, or more, heavy sweet cream**

Place metal blade in food processor. Add spinach, and puree. Melt butter in a large saucepan and spoon spinach into hot butter. Cook, stirring, for 3 minutes. Stir in flour and continue cooking, stirring, for another 3 to 5 minutes. Add seasonings and stir in cream gradually. Bring to a simmer and cook over low heat for 5 to 10 minutes. Correct seasoning and add more cream if you wish.

**Serves:** 4 to 6

# Jerry's Potato Chips

**½ cup, or more, cooking oil**
**2 pounds potatoes, peeled**
**Salt**

Heat ¼ cup of the oil in a large skillet.*

If your processor comes with different slicing discs, use the ultra-thin slicing disc to slice potatoes. Or use the slicing disc that comes with your machine. Slice potatoes and rinse slices in cold water. Dry thoroughly on paper towels.

When oil is hot and bubbling slightly, slip potato slices into skillet, a few at a time. Fry potatoes in batches until potatoes are crisp and golden brown. Add more oil as necessary. Drain potatoes on paper towels, sprinkle with salt, and keep warm in a 250-degree oven until all chips are fried and you are ready to serve them.

**Serves:** 6

* Potatoes may also be cooked in a deep-fat fryer. Heat oil to a temperature of 375 to 400 degrees. Fill basket of deep-fat fryer with potatoes. Dip in and out of hot oil until bubbling occurs. Continue in-and-out motion until bubbling stops.

When bubbling stops, allow potatoes to remain in basket, immersed in oil, until potatoes are golden brown. Drain potatoes on paper towels, salt, and serve at once.

# Doubly Delicious Baked Potatoes with Caviar

*We are indebted to Mr. Craig Claiborne, who inspired this recipe. Indeed, a whole world of people who like delicious food are indebted to Mr. Claiborne, for this and other fine cooking inventions.*

**8 Idaho baking potatoes**
**¼ pound, or more, butter**
**3 scallions, each one cut into 3 pieces**
**1 cup milk**
**½ cup heavy sweet cream**
**½ cup sour cream**
**Salt and freshly ground white pepper**
**8 ounces black caviar, or whitefish roe**

Bake potatoes for 1 hour, or until tender, in a preheated oven of 350 degrees. Slice 1 inch, lengthwise, off the tops of the potatoes. Place metal blade in food processor and scoop potato pulp from shells into processor. If your processor has a small bowl, puree potatoes in two steps. If it has a large bowl, puree all potatoes at one time. Add butter and scallions to potatoes and pulse on and off once. Scrape down sides of bowl and add all other ingredients, except for caviar, to processor. Pulse on and off, scraping down mixture from sides of bowl. Do not overprocess, or potatoes will have an unpleasant pastelike consistency. Add more butter or cream if you wish. Spoon potato puree back into bottom half of potato shells and place these stuffed potatoes in a baking dish. Before serving, place in preheated 400-degree oven and heat thoroughly. Remove hot potatoes from oven and garnish each potato with a tablespoonful of caviar.

**Serves:** 8

# Mother's Potato Pancakes

**4 potatoes, peeled**
**1 small onion, peeled**
**1 egg**
**2 tablespoons all-purpose flour**
**Salt and freshly ground black pepper to taste**
**Butter or oil for frying**

Place shredding disc in food processor. Shred potatoes and onion. Remove shredding disc from processor and replace with metal blade. Add egg, flour, and seasonings to processor. Process potato mixture until all ingredients are thoroughly combined. Spoon potato pancake mixture into a bowl.

Heat butter or oil in a large skillet and drop tablespoonfuls of batter into skillet. Press back of spoon down on each pancake to make it thin. Fry on both sides until crispy and brown. Serve at once.

**Serves:** 3 to 4

# Potato Cheese Casserole

**1 three-ounce package cream cheese**
**¼ pound Cheddar cheese, cut into cubes**
**1 cup creamed cottage cheese**
**2 tablespoons butter**
**¼ cup milk**
**1½ pounds potatoes, peeled, cubed, cooked, and drained**
**2 teaspoons dried chives**
**3 sprigs parsley**
**½ teaspoon white pepper**
**Mild paprika**

Place metal blade in food processor. Add all cheeses, butter, and milk to processor and pulse on and off, scraping down sides of bowl, until cheese is finely chopped. Add potatoes and all seasonings except paprika to processor. Continue processing, pulsing on and off and scraping down sides of bowl until ingredients are smoothly blended. Do not overprocess, or potatoes will have a pastelike consistency. Spoon potato mixture into a buttered 1-quart baking dish. Sprinkle paprika on top and bake in a preheated 350-degree oven for 30 to 40 minutes or until hot.

**Serves:** 6

# Sweet Potato Pudding

**4 baked sweet potatoes**
**1 cup firmly packed brown sugar**
**½ cup melted butter**
**4 egg yolks**
**2 teaspoons grated lemon rind**
**1 cup orange juice**
**4 egg whites**
**½ teaspoon cream of tartar**

Place metal blade in food processor. Scoop sweet potato pulp out of skins into food processor. Gradually add all ingredients, except egg whites and cream of tartar, and puree until all ingredients are thoroughly blended. Spoon mixture into a buttered baking or soufflé dish.

If your machine comes with a special accessory for beating egg whites, place beater and egg whites in processor, add cream of tartar, and beat egg whites until thick. Or use a hand beater and beat egg whites with cream of tartar until thick. Fold egg white mixture into sweet potato mixture. Place baking dish in a preheated 350-degree oven for 1 hour.

**Serves:** 4 to 6

# South-of-the-Border Salad

**1 head iceberg lettuce**
**1 fifteen-ounce can garbanzos, or chick peas, drained**
**⅓ cup olive oil**
**2 tablespoons wine vinegar**
**1 clove garlic, peeled**
**3 stalks celery, each stalk cut into 3 pieces**
**4 scallions, each scallion cut into 3 pieces**
**Salt and freshly ground black pepper to taste**
**½ cup croutons, sautéed in oil until crisp**

Core, rinse, and drain lettuce. Place shredding disc in food processor and shred lettuce. Remove to salad bowl. Add garbanzos. Place metal blade in processor. Add oil and vinegar to processor and, with machine on, drop garlic through feed tube. Process until dressing is blended. Add celery and scallions to processor and chop coarsely.

Spoon dressing-vegetable mixture over lettuce and garbanzos. Mix well. Season with salt and pepper and garnish with croutons. Serve at once or lettuce will wilt in dressing.

**Serves:** 6

# Steamed Peas with Lettuce and Onions

**1 medium head iceberg lettuce**
**2 cups water**
**Salt**
**1 pound small white pearl onions, peeled**
**1 ten-ounce package frozen green peas**
**⅛ teaspoon nutmeg**
**½ teaspoon dried tarragon, crumbled**
**4 tablespoons melted butter**

Core, rinse, and drain lettuce. Place shredding disc in food processor, and shred lettuce. Reserve. Heat water, with 1 teaspoon salt, to boiling in a 2½-quart saucepan. Add onions and cook covered 10 to 15 minutes or until onions are almost tender.

Place vegetable steamer basket in saucepan over onions. Add peas to basket and sprinkle with salt. Cover and steam 8 minutes. Uncover and add shredded lettuce to steamer basket and steam 2 to 3 minutes or until thoroughly heated.

Place lettuce in center of serving dish and arrange peas and drained onions on lettuce. Add nutmeg and tarragon to melted butter and drizzle over peas.

**Serves:** 4 to 6

# Zucchini in Sour Cream and Dill Sauce

**8 medium zucchini, peeled**
**1 small onion, peeled**
**8 sprigs fresh dill**
**¼ pound butter**
**Salt and freshly ground white pepper to taste**
**Juice of one lemon**
**2 tablespoons sugar, or more, to taste**
**2 teaspoons all-purpose flour**
**2 cups sour cream**
**½ teaspoon mild paprika**

Place slicing disc in food processor. Slice zucchini, remove from processor, and reserve. Place metal blade in food processor. Add onion and dill to processor and chop coarsely. Melt butter in a saucepan and add zucchini, onion, and dill. Season with salt and white pepper. Cover saucepan and cook over medium heat until zucchini is firm to tender, and not mushy. This can take approximately 15 to 20 minutes. Sprinkle lemon juice over zucchini, add sugar, and cook for another 2 minutes, stirring. Stir flour into sour cream until well blended. Gradually add sour cream mixture to zucchini, stirring. Stir in paprika. Cook, over low heat, until sauce thickens slightly, about another 5 to 10 minutes.

**Serves:** 6 to 8

# Baked Vegetables 'n' Spoonbread

**BAKED VEGETABLES**

**3 cloves garlic, peeled**
**¼ cup melted butter**
**2 teaspoons all-purpose flour**
**1 teaspoon salt**
**¼ teaspoon lemon pepper**
**⅛ teaspoon rosemary, crushed**
**½ pound potatoes, peeled**
**1 small onion, peeled**
**2 medium, firm, ripe tomatoes**
**1 pound fresh peas, shelled**

**SPOONBREAD TOPPING**

**4 ounces Cheddar cheese**
**1⅓ cup milk**
**1 tablespoon butter**
**½ cup cornmeal**
**2 eggs, separated**
**1 teaspoon salt**

*To Make Baked Vegetables:*

Place metal blade in food processor. With machine on, drop garlic through feed tube. Process until chopped. Remove garlic and combine with butter, flour, salt, lemon pepper, and rosemary. Place slicing disc in food processor. Slice potatoes and remove and reserve. Slice onion and remove and reserve. If your processor has an expanded feed tube, you can slice tomatoes whole. If tube is too small, cut tomatoes in half. Slice tomatoes and reserve. Layer vegetables in a 7½-cup soufflé dish. Start with peas, top with potatoes, onions, and tomato slices. Spoon garlic-butter mixture over each layer. Cover tightly with foil. Bake in a preheated 350-degree oven for 25 minutes. While vegetables are baking, prepare Spoonbread Topping.

*To Make Spoonbread Topping:*

Place shredding disc in food processor. Shred cheese, remove, and reserve. Combine milk, butter, and cornmeal in a small saucepan. Bring to a full boil, stirring constantly, and cook until thick. Remove from heat.

Beat egg yolks slightly. Stir a little of hot cornmeal mixture into yolks, then combine with remaining cornmeal mixture. Stir in Cheddar cheese and salt. If your machine has an attachment to beat egg whites, beat until stiff. If not, use a hand beater or whisk to beat egg whites until stiff. Fold beaten egg whites into cornmeal mixture.

Remove baking dish from oven. Uncover and spread Spoonbread over vegetables. Return to oven and bake, uncovered, for 35 to 40 minutes or until topping is puffed and brown. The point of a knife inserted in center of Spoonbread should come out clean. Serve at once.

**Serves:** 4

# Stuffings

*Not vegetables, exactly, but stuffings often do take the place of a vegetable course. Here, then, are two stuffing recipes to be prepared in the food processor.*

## Fruit Stuffing

**6 slices white bread, broken in pieces**
**1 cup mixed dried fruits**
**1 apple, peeled, cored, and cut into quarters**
**1 teaspoon salt**
**½ teaspoon poultry seasoning**
**4 tablespoons butter**
**¾ cup orange juice**
**½ cup raisins**

Place metal blade in food processor. Add bread and process until bread is in crumbs. Remove and reserve. Add mixed fruits and apple to processor. Pulse on and off until fruits are diced. Return bread to processor and add remaining ingredients. Process until all ingredients are combined.

**Yield:** 2 cups stuffing

# Prune Walnut Stuffing

**6 slices white bread, broken in pieces**
**1 cup pitted prunes**
**1 cup walnuts**
**1 stalk celery, cut into 3 pieces**
**4 sprigs parsley**
**½ cup orange juice**
**4 tablespoons butter**
**1 teaspoon salt**
**¼ teaspoon freshly ground black pepper**

Place metal blade in food processor. Add bread and process until bread is in crumbs. Remove and reserve. Add prunes, walnuts, celery, and parsley to processor. Pulse on and off until ingredients are diced. Return bread to processor. Add remaining ingredients and process until all ingredients are combined.

**Yield:** 3 cups stuffing

# CHINESE FAVORITES

Chinese cooking requires a great deal of slicing, chopping, and shredding. Now, thanks to the food processor, much of the preparation for this deliciously different cuisine can be accomplished quickly and easily.

The recipes in this section were adapted for the processor, and if you want to adapt some of your favorite Chinese dishes, remember the following:

- Partially freeze meat, chicken, and fish to facilitate slicing.

- The processor will chop, but it will not create a neat dice. However, most Chinese recipes work well with vegetables that are roughly chopped.

- If you have a recipe that calls for shredded meat, substitute sliced meat. If you want narrower strips of meat, slice, remove the meat from the processor, and slice once again.

- The processor works especially well when a recipe calls for finely minced or mashed ingredients.

Chinese cooking does require many steps. Vegetables often have to be sliced and cooked separately. However, the processor will do the slicing or chopping so quickly that you'll be able to create delicious Chinese dishes without having to stand beside a cutting board for hours.

# Pork and Scallions

**1 pound boneless pork loin**
**12 scallions**
**3 large carrots, cleaned and scraped**
**2 cloves garlic, peeled**
**1 tablespoon sugar**
**1 tablespoon cornstarch**
**2 tablespoons dry sherry wine**
**2 tablespoons soy sauce**
**3 to 4 tablespoons peanut oil**

Cut pork in chunks to fit feed tube. Wrap pork and place in freezer for 1 to 1½ hours, or until firm, but not frozen.

Place slicing disc in food processor. Fit pork in feed tube and slice. Remove meat, place in a bowl, and reserve. Slice scallions and carrots and reserve. Place metal blade in food processor. With machine on, drop garlic through feed tube. Add remaining ingredients, except for oil, to processor, and process until combined. Pour garlic-sauce mixture over pork and marinate for 30 minutes. Remove meat from marinade with slotted spoon. Reserve marinade.

Heat oil in a wok or large skillet. Stir-fry pork slices quickly. Add carrots and scallions to skillet and stir-fry quickly, about 1 minute. Add marinade to skillet. Simmer about 2 minutes or until liquid thickens.

**Serves:** 4 to 6

# Beef and Crispy Red Radishes

**1 pound lean beef (top round)**
**12 red radishes, washed not peeled**
**6 scallions**
**2 cloves garlic, peeled**
**1 tablespoon cornstarch**
**2 tablespoons soy sauce**
**1 tablespoon brown sugar**
**2 tablespoons wine vinegar**
**½ cup water**
**3 to 4 tablespoons peanut oil**

Cut beef into chunks to fit feed tube. Wrap beef and place in freezer for 1 to 1½ hours or until firm but not frozen.

Place slicing disc in food processor. Fit beef into feed tube and slice. Remove meat from processor and reserve. Slice radishes and scallions. Remove and reserve. Place metal blade in food processor. With machine on, drop garlic through feed tube. Add remaining ingredients, except for oil, and process until combined.

Heat oil in a wok or large skillet. Stir-fry beef until beef is no longer red. Using a slotted spoon, remove beef from skillet. Add garlic-sauce mixture to skillet. Heat, stirring constantly, until sugar dissolves. Add beef to pan and cook, stirring, an additional 2 minutes. Add radishes and scallions to pan and cook, stirring until vegetables are hot. Do not overcook, as vegetables should remain crisp.

**Serves:** 4

# Seafood Cakes with Water Chestnuts

**1 pound combination of shrimp, crab, fish fillets**
**1 five-ounce can water chestnuts, drained**
**2 slices white bread, broken into pieces**
**1 clove garlic, peeled**
**1 small carrot, cleaned, scraped, and cut into chunks**
**1 stalk celery, cut in half**
**3 tablespoons oyster sauce**
**1 tablespoon soy sauce**
**1 egg, lightly beaten**
**Cornstarch**
**Peanut oil**

Place metal blade in food processor. Add seafood, water chestnuts, bread, garlic, carrot, celery, oyster sauce, and soy sauce. Process until all ingredients are thoroughly blended. Form seafood mixture into small, flat cakes. Dip crab cakes into beaten egg and then lightly into cornstarch.

Heat oil and, using a slotted spoon, place crab cakes in oil. Fry until golden. Drain. Serve with Basic Sweet 'n' Spicy Sauce (see recipe on page 194).

**Serves:** 2 to 3

# Spicy Chicken and Peanuts

**2 chicken breasts, boned, skin removed**
**2 scallions**
**1 stalk celery**
**1 clove garlic, peeled**
**1 thin slice ginger root, peeled**
**2 teaspoons cornstarch**
**3 tablespoons soy sauce**
**2 tablespoons dry sherry**
**¼ teaspoon hot pepper oil or cayenne pepper**
**2 to 4 tablespoons peanut oil**
**½ cup shelled peanuts**

Trim chicken breasts to fit feed tube. Wrap chicken and place in freezer for 45 minutes to 1 hour or until firm but not frozen.

Place slicing disc in food processor. Fit chicken into feed tube and slice. Remove chicken from processor and reserve. Slice scallions and celery. Remove and reserve. Place metal blade in food processor. With machine on, drop garlic and ginger root through feed tube. Add remaining ingredients, except peanut oil and peanuts. Process until combined.

Heat oil in a wok or large skillet. Stir-fry chicken until it is no longer pink, about 3 minutes. Using a slotted spoon, remove from skillet. Reserve. Add more oil as needed. Stir-fry scallions and celery for about 2 minutes. Remove and reserve. Add garlic-sauce mixture to skillet. Heat, stirring constantly, until mixture thickens. Add chicken, vegetables, and peanuts to skillet. Heat, stirring constantly, for about 1 minute, or until hot.

**Serves:** 4 to 6

# Pork and Chicken Soong

**½ pound boneless pork loin, cut into 1-inch pieces**
**1 chicken breast, boned, skin removed, cut into chunks**
**1 five-ounce can water chestnuts, drained**
**½ cup bamboo shoots**
**2 cloves garlic, peeled**
**3 tablespoons peanut oil**
**2 tablespoons soy sauce**
**Freshly ground black pepper to taste**
**1 cup chicken broth**
**1 tablespoon cornstarch**
**3 tablespoons water**
**1 head iceberg lettuce**
**Hoisin sauce**

Place metal blade in food processor. Add pork, chicken, water chestnuts, bamboo shoots, and garlic. Process until meat and vegetables are minced. Remove and reserve.

Heat oil in a wok or large skillet. Stir-fry pork, chicken, and vegetables for 2 to 3 minutes. Add soy sauce, pepper, and chicken broth to skillet. Stir to combine all ingredients and cover pan. Cook for 10 minutes. Combine cornstarch and water, stirring to form a paste. Add cornstarch mixture to pan and cook until sauce has thickened.

Separate lettuce into leaves and serve two or more leaves to each person. Spoon approximately 2 tablespoons chicken mixture onto each lettuce leaf. Top with a teaspoon of Hoisin sauce. Roll, and eat with fingers.

**Serves:** 6 to 8

# Chicken with Bean Sprouts

**2 whole chicken breasts, boned, skin removed**
**¼ pound mushrooms**
**2 onions, peeled**
**2 stalks celery**
**1 clove garlic, peeled**
**3 tablespoons soy sauce**
**1 tablespoon dry sherry**
**2 teaspoons cornstarch**
**1 teaspoon brown sugar**
**3 to 4 tablespoons peanut oil**
**1 pound bean sprouts**

Cut chicken breasts to fit feed tube. Wrap and place in freezer for 45 minutes to 1 hour or until firm but not frozen.

Place slicing disc in food processor. Fit chicken into feed tube and slice. Remove from processor and reserve. Slice mushrooms, onions, and celery. Remove and reserve. Place metal blade in food processor. With machine on, drop garlic through feed tube and add soy sauce, sherry, cornstarch, and brown sugar and process until combined.

Heat oil in a wok or large skillet. Stir-fry chicken for 2 to 3 minutes. Remove and reserve. Add vegetables to skillet and stir-fry about 2 minutes. Add garlic-sauce mixture to skillet and simmer about 2 minutes or until thickened. Return chicken to skillet. Heat about 2 minutes.

**Serves:** 4 to 6

# Fish Steak with Bamboo Shoots and Pineapple

**1 pound fish steaks (cod, halibut, or swordfish)**
**3 tablespoons soy sauce**
**2 tablespoons dry sherry**
**¼ teaspoon Tabasco**
**1 small onion, peeled**
**2 eggs**
**2 tablespoons cornstarch**
**1 sixteen-ounce can pineapple chunks, undrained**
**4 tablespoons peanut oil**
**1 cup bamboo shoots**

Cut fish steaks to fit feed tube. Wrap fish and place in freezer for 45 minutes to 1 hour, or until fish steaks are firm but not frozen.

Combine soy sauce, sherry, and Tabasco. Reserve. Place slicing disc in food processor. Slice fish. Remove and reserve. Slice onion. Remove and reserve.

Marinate fish in soy sauce mixture for 20 to 30 minutes. Combine eggs and cornstarch, and blend until a batter is formed. Dip marinated fish slices in batter, coating thoroughly. Combine the remaining batter with pineapple. Mix thoroughly. Reserve.

Heat oil in a wok or large skillet. Add fish and brown, turning from side to side. Remove, and drain fish slices. Add onion and bamboo shoots to skillet and stir-fry for 3 minutes. Remove and reserve. Add pineapple-batter mixture to skillet, simmer, stirring until sauce thickens. Return fish and vegetables to the skillet with pineapple mixture. Stir well to combine. Heat about 2 minutes. Serve.

**Serves:** 4

# Sliced Beef Szechuan

**1½ pounds lean beef (top round)**
**4 carrots, cleaned and scraped**
**4 stalks celery**
**4 scallions**
**4 cloves garlic, peeled**
**1 thin slice ginger root, peeled**
**3 to 4 tablespoons peanut oil**
**2 teaspoons hot bean paste**
**1 teaspoon dry sherry**
**1 tablespoon soy sauce**
**1 teaspoon sugar**
**1 teaspoon sesame oil**
**1 teaspoon Worcestershire Sauce**
**1½ teaspoons ground Szechuan pepper**

Cut beef into chunks to fit feed tube. Wrap meat and place in freezer for 1½ to 2 hours, or until firm but not frozen.

Place slicing disc in food processor. Slice beef. Remove and reserve. Slice carrots, celery, and scallions. Remove and reserve. Place metal blade in food processor. With machine on, drop garlic and ginger root through feed tube. Process until chopped.

Heat 2 tablespoons oil in wok or large skillet. Stir-fry meat for 3 minutes or until it loses its red color. Remove and reserve. Add 1 tablespoon of oil to skillet. Stir-fry carrots, celery, and scallions for about 2 minutes. Remove and reserve. Add remaining oil to skillet. Add garlic, ginger root, and hot bean paste to skillet, and stir-fry for 2 minutes. Add meat, vegetables, and all remaining ingredients, except for Szechuan pepper, to skillet. Stir-fry for 3 minutes, or until all ingredients are thoroughly combined and hot. Stir in Szechuan pepper.

**Serves:** 4 to 6

# Moo Shoo Pork Pancakes

*Chinese pancakes, also known as doilies, are the right accompaniment to Moo Shoo Pork. They are also served traditionally with Peking Duck. Allow each guest two to three pancakes, and serve with a platter of Moo Shoo Pork. Let your guests help themselves, and remind them that Moo Shoo Pork is best when rolled and eaten with the fingers.*

**FILLING**

**½ pound boneless pork loin**
**¼ cup lily buds**
**2 tablespoons cloud ear mushrooms**
**4 tablespoons soy sauce**
**1 teaspoon sugar**
**¼ cup water**
**2 thin slices ginger root, peeled**
**1 scallion**
**½ cup bamboo shoots**
**4 tablespoons peanut oil**
**2 eggs, beaten**
**Salt to taste**
**Dash of cayenne pepper or hot pepper oil (optional)**

**PANCAKES**

**2 cups flour**
**1 cup boiling water**
**Peanut oil**

*To Make Filling:*

Cut pork in chunks to fit feed tube. Wrap meat and place in freezer for 1 to 1½ hours, or until firm but not frozen.

Using two separate bowls, soak lily buds and cloud ear mushrooms in water for 30 minutes. Combine soy sauce, sugar, and water. Reserve.

Place slicing disc in food processor. Fit meat in feed tube. Slice. Remove and slice once again. Remove and reserve. Marinate meat in soy sauce mixture for 10 minutes. Place metal blade in food processor. With machine on, drop ginger root through feed tube. Process until chopped. Add cloud ear mushrooms, lily buds, scallion, and bamboo shoots to processor. Process 10 seconds or until chopped.

Heat 2 tablespoons oil in a wok or large skillet. Add eggs and scramble, stirring. Add salt. Eggs should remain moist, not dry. Remove and reserve. Add pork to skillet and cook, stirring, until pork is no longer pink. Heat remaining oil in skillet. Add ginger root, mushrooms, lily buds, and bamboo shoots to skillet and stir-fry for 2 minutes. Return scrambled eggs to skillet with vegetables, pork, salt, and pepper, and stir-fry until all ingredients are hot and thoroughly combined. Serve Moo Shoo Pork filling with Pancakes, allowing all guests to roll their own pancakes.

*To Make Pancakes:*

Place metal blade in food processor. Add flour to processor. With machine on, pour water through feed tube. Process until dough forms a ball. Remove dough to a lightly floured board. Cover dough with a damp towel and allow to stand for 15 minutes. Roll and stretch dough to form a long, thin strand, about 2 inches in diameter. Cut the dough into slices that are approximately ½- to 1-inch thick. Roll each slice into a 1-inch round, approximately ¼ inch thick. Brush one side of each round with oil. Place one round of dough on top of another round, the oiled sides touching. Roll each pair of rounds into one thin disc, about 4 to 5 inches in diameter.

Heat a skillet, but do not use any oil, and slip one disc into the skillet at a time. Cook approximately 1 minute on each side. Dough should only be light brown. When each dough round is cooked, remove from skillet and separate at once into 2 pancakes. You will have between 12 and 15 pancakes.

**Serves:** 4 to 6

# Vegetables Chinese Style

**2 carrots, cleaned and scraped**
**6 scallions**
**1 zucchini**
**1 six-ounce can water chestnuts**
**1 clove garlic, peeled**
**½ cup chicken broth**
**1 tablespoon cornstarch**
**3 tablespoons soy sauce**
**¼ teaspoon ground ginger**
**3 tablespoons peanut oil**
**½ pound fresh snow peas or 1 ten-ounce package frozen snow peas, thawed**
**1 sixteen-ounce can bean sprouts, drained**

Place slicing blade in food processor. Slice carrots, scallions, zucchini and water chestnuts. Remove and reserve. Place metal blade in food processor. With machine on, drop garlic through feed tube. Process until chopped. Add broth, cornstarch, soy sauce, and ginger. Process until combined.

Heat oil in wok or large skillet. Stir-fry sliced vegetables and snow peas 2 to 3 minutes. Add garlic-sauce mixture to skillet and simmer for 2 minutes, or until sauce thickens. Stir in bean sprouts. Heat 1 minute or until hot.

**Serves:** 4 to 6

# Chinese Fish Balls with Ginger

**1 clove garlic, peeled**
**1 thin slice ginger root, peeled**
**2 scallions**
**1 pound fish fillets**
**1 egg**
**1 tablespoon dry sherry**
**1 teaspoon cornstarch**
**1 teaspoon salt**
**½ teaspoon freshly ground black pepper**
**2 tablespoons water**
**Peanut oil**

Place metal blade in food processor. With machine on, drop garlic and ginger through feed tube. Process until chopped. Add scallions, fish, egg, sherry, cornstarch, salt, pepper, and water. Process until all ingredients are smooth and thoroughly blended. Shape fish mixture into ten 2-inch fishballs.

Heat 2 inches of oil in a wok or large skillet. Place fishballs in skillet. Fry 5 to 8 minutes, or until golden brown. Serve with Basic Sweet 'n' Spicy Sauce (see page 194) or with a mixture of duck sauce and mustard.

**Serves:** 3 to 4

# Sliced Beef and Snow Peas

**1 pound lean beef (top round)**
**1 medium onion, peeled**
**1 clove garlic, peeled**
**1 thin slice ginger root, peeled**
**3 tablespoons soy sauce**
**½ cup beef broth**
**½ cup water**
**1 tablespoon dry sherry**
**1 teaspoon sugar**
**1 tablespoon cornstarch**
**3 to 4 tablespoons peanut oil**
**1 ten-ounce package frozen snow peas, thawed, or ¾ pound fresh snow peas**

Cut beef into chunks to fit feed tube. Wrap beef and place in freezer for 1 to 1½ hours, or until firm but not frozen.

Place slicing disc in food processor. Slice beef and reserve. Slice onion and reserve. Place metal blade in food processor. With machine on, drop garlic and ginger root through feed tube. Add soy sauce, beef broth, water, sherry, sugar, and cornstarch. Process until combined.

Heat 3 tablespoons of oil in a wok or large skillet. Stir-fry beef until it is no longer red. Remove and reserve. Add remaining oil to skillet; stir-fry onions for 2 minutes. Remove and reserve. Add snow peas to skillet and stir-fry for 2 minutes. Return meat and onions to skillet and heat, stirring constantly, for about 2 minutes. Add garlic-sauce mixture to skillet. Heat, stirring constantly, until mixture begins to thicken.

**Serves:** 6

# Pork with Sweet Bean Paste

**1 pound boneless pork loin**
**12 scallions**
**2 tablespoons soy sauce**
**1 teaspoon dry sherry**
**3 tablespoons water**
**1 teaspoon cornstarch**
**3 tablespoons peanut oil**
**1⅓ tablespoons sweet bean paste**
**½ tablespoon dry sherry**
**2 teaspoons sugar**

Cut pork into pieces to fit feed tube. Wrap pork and place in freezer for 1½ to 2 hours or until firm but not frozen.

Place slicing disc in food processor. Slice pork. Remove and reserve. Place shredding blade in food processor. Shred scallions. Remove to a serving platter. Combine one tablespoon soy sauce, sherry, water, and cornstarch and pour over pork. Marinate for 20 minutes.

Heat 3 tablespoons oil in a wok or large skillet. Add pork and marinade to skillet. Stir-fry for 3 minutes, or until pork is cooked. Remove and reserve. Combine sweet bean paste with ½ tablespoon sherry, one tablespoon soy sauce, and sugar. Add mixture to skillet. Simmer, stirring constantly, for 2 minutes. Return pork to skillet, stirring well to coat meat. Simmer for 2 minutes. Spoon onto shredded scallions and serve.

**Serves:** 4 to 6

# Scallops Peking

**1 pound sea scallops**
**1 small onion, peeled**
**1 clove garlic, peeled**
**2 tablespoons catsup**
**2 tablespoons soy sauce**
**2 tablespoons wine vinegar**
**2 teaspoons brown sugar**
**1 tablespoon dry sherry**
**1 tablespoon cornstarch**
**3 tablespoons water**
**3 tablespoons peanut oil**

Wrap scallops and place in freezer for 45 minutes to 1 hour or until scallops are firm but not frozen.

Place slicing disc in food processor. Slice scallops. Remove and reserve. Slice onion and garlic. Combine onion, garlic, catsup, soy sauce, vinegar, sugar, and sherry in a small saucepan. Bring sauce to a simmer. Combine cornstarch and water, mixing thoroughly, and add gradually to mixture in saucepan. Cook another minute or two until sauce thickens. Reserve.

Heat oil in a wok or a large skillet, add scallops, and stir-fry until lightly browned, about 3 minutes. Remove and drain. Place scallops on a serving platter. Reheat sauce and pour over scallops.

**Serves:** 4

# Pork Lo Mein

**1 pound boneless pork loin**
**1 pound linguine**
**2 tablespoons vegetable oil**
**1 large onion, peeled**
**3 carrots, peeled, cleaned and scraped**
**3 cucumbers, peeled**
**1 pound cabbage, cut into wedges**
**5 cloves garlic, peeled**
**⅓ cup soy sauce**
**¼ cup water**
**1 tablespoon sugar**
**1 tablespoon dry sherry**
**1 tablespoon cornstarch**
**3 to 4 tablespoons peanut oil**

Cut pork into chunks to fit feed tube. Wrap meat and place in freezer for 1 to 1½ hours, or until firm but not frozen. Cook linguine *al dente,* or slightly firm to the bite. Toss with vegetable oil and reserve.

Place slicing disc in food processor. Slice pork. Remove and reserve. Slice onions. Remove and reserve. Place shredding disc in food processor. Shred carrots, cucumbers, and cabbage. Remove and reserve. Place metal blade in food processor. With machine on, drop garlic through feed tube. Add all remaining ingredients except oil, and process until combined.

Heat oil in a wok or large skillet. Stir-fry sliced pork for about 2 minutes. Remove and reserve. Stir-fry onions, carrots, cucumbers, and cabbage for 2 minutes. Remove and reserve. Add garlic-sauce mixture to skillet; simmer 2 to 3 minutes or until sauce thickens. Return meat and vegetables to skillet. Heat until hot, about 2 minutes. Serve over linguine.

**Serves:** 4 to 6

# Pork and Mushrooms with Oyster Sauce

**1 pound boneless pork loin**
**¼ pound mushrooms**
**2 stalks celery**
**6 scallions**
**1 clove garlic, peeled**
**1 tablespoon cornstarch**
**2 tablespoons soy sauce**
**2 tablespoons oyster sauce**
**½ cup chicken broth**
**1 tablespoon dry sherry**
**4 tablespoons peanut oil**

Cut pork into pieces to fit feed tube. Wrap pork and place in freezer for 1 to 1½ hours or until firm but not frozen.

Place slicing disc in food processor. Slice pork. Remove and reserve. Slice mushrooms, celery, and scallions. Remove and reserve. Place metal blade in food processor. With machine on, drop garlic through feed tube. Add remaining ingredients, except oil, and process until combined.

Heat 2 tablespoons of oil in a wok or large skillet. Add meat and stir-fry until lightly browned, about 4 to 5 minutes. Remove and reserve. Add remaining oil to skillet. Stir-fry mushrooms, celery, and scallions for 3 minutes. Remove and reserve. Add garlic-sauce mixture to skillet. Heat, stirring constantly, until mixture begins to thicken. Return meat and vegetables to skillet. Heat for 1 minute, stirring to combine.

**Serves:** 6

# Basic Sweet 'n' Spicy Sauce

**½ cup light brown sugar**
**½ cup vinegar**
**½ cup water**
**2 tablespoons soy sauce**
**2 tablespoons catsup**
**1½ tablespoons cornstarch**
**½ cup water**
**1 clove garlic, peeled**
**1 green pepper, seeded**
**1 carrot, cleaned and scraped**
**1 celery stalk**
**2 scallions**
**2 tablespoons oil**

Combine sugar, vinegar, water, soy sauce, and catsup in a small saucepan. Bring to a simmer and cook, stirring, for about 3 minutes or until sugar dissolves. Mix cornstarch and water in a bowl, blending well. Add to vinegar-sugar mixture, stirring well to combine. Bring sauce to a simmer and cook for about 2 minutes, stirring constantly, until mixture thickens. Place slicing blade in food processor. Slice garlic, green pepper, carrot, celery, and scallions.

Heat oil in a wok or large skillet. Add vegetables to pan and cook, stirring until vegetables are slightly softened, about 2 to 3 minutes. Do not overcook. Vegetables should be crisp, not limp. Add vegetables to sauce. Heat about 2 minutes before serving. Serve over fish, pork, or poultry.

**Yield:** Approximately 2½ cups

# Beef Sukiyaki

*Not Chinese, but a favorite with people who like Japanese cooking, is sukiyaki. With the food processor, this delectable dish can now be easily added to your cooking repertoire.*

**1 pound lean beef (top round)**
**3 medium onions, peeled**
**3 stalks celery**
**¼ pound mushrooms**
**3 tablespoons peanut oil**
**3 cups spinach**
**½ cup bamboo shoots**
**¾ cup beef broth**
**½ cup soy sauce**
**1 tablespoon sugar**
**1 cake soy bean curd (tofu) cut into 1×1×1-inch cubes**
**½ cup cellophane noodles**

Cut beef into chunks to fit feed tube. Wrap beef and place in freezer for 1 to 1½ hours or until firm but not frozen.

Place slicing disc in food processor. Slice beef. Remove and reserve. Slice onions, celery, and mushrooms. Remove and reserve.

Heat oil in wok or large skillet. Stir-fry onions, celery, mushrooms, spinach, and bamboo shoots for 2 to 3 minutes. Arrange beef slices over the vegetables. Add broth, soy sauce, sugar, bean curd, and cellophane noodles to skillet. Cook uncovered over low heat, stirring once or twice, until beef is tender and vegetables are cooked but crisp. Serve with rice.

**Serves:** 4 to 6

# BREADS AND PASTRIES

Years ago people were admired if they had a fine hand or a delicate touch with pastry dough. But now, thanks to food processors, every pie shell can be flaky, every tart a delicate mouthful.

Today's processors also make quick work of bread doughs. Processors vary in size. Some of the older machines, as well as some of the new ones, have a smaller capacity, and can only prepare one piecrust, or enough dough for one loaf of bread, at a time. However, the machines work so quickly that it's only a matter of a few minutes to prepare another piecrust, or dough for another loaf of bread.

A loaf of homemade bread presented with a pot of sweet butter makes a meal something special, while a pie or a quiche made from scratch will delight all who come to your table.

If you have a food processor with a large-capacity bowl, take a look at the next section of this book which is devoted to bread and pastry recipes developed especially for those machines. And do look at that section no matter what size your machine—a handy table is included so that the recipes can be adapted for all food processors.

# Banana Bread

**¼ pound butter, cut into 6 or 8 pieces**
**1 cup sugar**
**2 eggs**
**4 very ripe bananas, peeled, each one cut into 3 pieces**
**2 cups all-purpose flour**
**1 teaspoon baking powder**
**1 teaspoon baking soda**
**¼ teaspoon salt**

Place metal blade in food processor. Add butter, sugar, and eggs to processor. Pulse on and off until all ingredients are blended. Add bananas and pulse on and off again until bananas are blended into mixture.

Combine flour, baking powder, baking soda, and salt, and add gradually to processor. Pulse on and off, scraping down sides of bowl with a spatula. Do not overprocess. Process only until flour disappears into other ingredients.

Spoon mixture into a greased 9×5×3-inch loaf pan. Bake in a preheated 350-degree oven for 1 hour.

**Yield:** 1 loaf

# Orange Marmalade Nut Bread

**½ cup orange marmalade**
**1 egg yolk**
**½ cup milk**
**1 tablespoon grated orange peel**
**½ cup shelled pecans**
**1 teaspoon salt**
**2 cups all-purpose flour**
**2 teaspoons baking powder**

Place metal blade in food processor. Add marmalade, egg yolk, milk, orange peel, pecans, and salt to processor. Pulse on and off until ingredients are blended. Combine flour and baking powder, and add to processor gradually. Pulse on and off, scraping mixture down from sides of bowl. Do not overprocess. Process only until flour disappears into other ingredients.

Spoon mixture into a buttered 9×5×3-inch loaf pan. Allow mixture to rest for 20 minutes. Bake in a preheated 350-degree oven for 45 minutes.

**Yield:** 1 loaf

# Spicy Raisin Tea Loaf

**¼ pound (or 1 stick) butter, cut into 6 or 8 pieces**
**½ cup sugar**
**½ cup light or dark molasses**
**2 eggs**
**⅔ cup milk**
**1 carrot, cleaned, scraped, and peeled and cut into 6 pieces**
**1 cup walnuts**
**½ cup dark raisins**
**1 teaspoon vanilla extract**
**1 cup all-purpose flour**
**1½ cups whole wheat flour**
**3 teaspoons baking powder**
**½ teaspoon each: cinnamon, nutmeg, and allspice**

Place metal blade in food processor. Add butter, sugar, molasses, eggs, milk, carrot, walnuts, raisins, and vanilla to processor. Pulse on and off until ingredients are blended. Add flours, baking powder, and spices gradually. Pulse on and off. Do not overprocess. Process only until flour disappears into other ingredients.

Spoon dough into a greased and floured 9×5×3-inch loaf pan. Bake in a preheated 350-degree oven for 1 hour or until loaf feels firm to the touch. Remove from pan and allow to cool. Serve in thin slices with butter, cream cheese, jam, or marmalade.

**Yield:** 1 loaf

# Pâté Brisée for Pies, Tarts, and Quiches

*There are a variety of fine recipes for* pâté brisée, *or French pastry dough. We offer a few recipes here, and with a bit of experimentation you will soon find your favorite. When working with* pâté brisée, *remember the following:*

*Flour varies in porosity, and you may find it necessary to adjust the recipe for less or more flour to create a dough with the proper consistency and texture.*

*If pastry dough does not form a ball as you're processing, add a bit more liquid. Be sure, however, to add the water in very small amounts.*

*Refrigerated* pâté brisée *dough is easier to work with, and we suggest you chill dough for at least 30 minutes before using.*

Pâté brisée *dough can be stored in the refrigerator for approximately two days and kept in the freezer for months.*

# Pâté Brisée I

**1⅓ cups all-purpose flour**
**¼ pound chilled sweet butter, cut into 6 to 8 pieces**
**1 teaspoon salt**
**2 to 3 tablespoons ice water**

Place metal blade in food processor. Add all ingredients, except ice water, to processor. Process until the mixture has the consistency of coarse meal. With the machine running, add water to the processor. Continue processing until mixture forms a ball. Refrigerate at least 30 minutes before using.

**Yield:** 1 nine-inch crust

## Pâté Brisée II

**2 cups all-purpose flour**
**¼ pound plus 2 tablespoons chilled butter, cut into 8 pieces**
**1 teaspoon salt**
**1 egg**
**1½ to 2 tablespoons ice water**

Place metal blade in food processor. Add all ingredients, except water, to processor. Process until the mixture has the consistency of coarse meal. With the machine running, add water to the processor. Continue processing until mixture forms a ball. Refrigerate at least 30 minutes before using.

**Yield:** 2 eight-inch crusts

## Pâté Brisée Sucrée I

**1¾ cups all-purpose flour**
**Pinch of salt**
**2 tablespoons sugar**
**¼ pound plus 2 tablespoons sweet butter, chilled and cut into 8 pieces**
**2 tablespoons vegetable shortening, chilled and cut into 2 pieces**
**3 to 4 tablespoons ice water**

Place metal blade in food processor. Add all ingredients, except water, to processor. Process until the mixture has the consistency of coarse meal. With the machine running, add water to the processor. Continue processing until mixture forms a ball. Refrigerate at least 30 minutes before using.

**Yield:** 2 eight-inch crusts

# Pâté Brisée Sucrée II

**1⅓ cups all-purpose flour**
**¼ pound sweet butter, chilled and cut into 6 or 8 pieces**
**Pinch of salt**
**1 tablespoon sugar**
**2 to 3 tablespoons ice water**

Place metal blade in food processor. Place all ingredients except ice water in food processor. Process until the mixture has the consistency of coarse meal. With the machine running, add water to the processor. Continue processing until mixture forms a ball. Refrigerate at least 30 minutes before using.

**Yield:** 1 nine-inch crust

# Pâté Brisée Sucrée III

**1¼ cups all-purpose flour**
**¼ pound chilled sweet butter, cut into 6 or 8 pieces**
**1 tablespoon sugar**
**¼ teaspoon salt**
**1 tablespoon ice water**
**1 egg**

Place metal blade in food processor. Add the first 4 ingredients to processor and process until the mixture has the consistency of coarse meal. With the machine running, add the water and the egg and continue processing until mixture forms a ball. Refrigerate at least 30 minutes before using.

**Yield:** 1 nine-inch crust

# All-American Piecrust Dough

**1 cup all-purpose flour**
**½ cup vegetable shortening**
**3 to 4 tablespoons ice water**

Place metal blade in food processor. Add flour and shortening and process until the mixture has the consistency of coarse meal. Add water and continue processing until dough forms a ball.

**Yield:** 1 nine-inch crust.

# Langosh

*Not many people have heard of Langosh, but it's a popular snack in Hungary, where it's served with wine or beer. When trying to explain this dish, Hungarians say that it's their answer to German pretzels or Italian pizza. It's certainly more unusual than either.*

**½ cup warm milk (105 to 115 degrees)**
**2 teaspoons yeast (½ of quarter-ounce envelope)**
**½ teaspoon sugar**
**4 medium potatoes, peeled, quartered, cooked and drained**
**1⅔ cups all-purpose flour**
**½ teaspoon salt**
**Vegetable oil for frying**
**Garlic salt**
**Hot paprika (optional)**

Place metal blade in food processor. Add warm milk to processor, and sprinkle yeast and sugar over milk. Allow to stand for 5 minutes. Add potatoes, flour, and salt to processor. Pulse on and off for 10 seconds, or until all ingredients are thoroughly blended. Remove blade from processor, and spoon dough into a well-greased bowl. Cover, and allow to rise in a warm, draft-free place for 45 minutes, or until dough has doubled in bulk. Stir dough down in bowl.

In a large, 12-inch skillet, heat oil over medium heat. Oil should be about ½ inch deep in pan. Spoon large tablespoonfuls of dough into frying pan. Dough will puff up. Fry over medium heat, removing Langosh and draining on paper towels. Langosh should be a light brown. Sprinkle with garlic salt and hot paprika, if you wish.

**Yield:** Approximately 20 Langosh

# Sour Cream Blueberry Muffins

**1 egg**
**1 cup sugar**
**1 cup sour cream**
**¼ cup vegetable oil**
**1¾ cup all-purpose flour**
**1 teaspoon baking soda**
**½ teaspoon salt**
**1 cup fresh or unthawed frozen blueberries**

Place metal blade in food processor. Add egg, sugar, sour cream, and vegetable oil to processor. Pulse on and off for 5 seconds, or until ingredients are thoroughly blended. Combine flour, baking soda, and salt. Add to processor. Pulse on and off once or twice, or just until ingredients are blended. Do not overprocess. Stir in blueberries and scrape down sides of bowl with spatula, combining all ingredients.

Spoon mixture into 12 greased, medium-sized (2¾-inch diameter) muffin cups. Fill ⅔ full. Bake in preheated 400-degree oven for 15 to 20 minutes, or until toothpick inserted in center comes out clean.

**Yield:** 12 muffins

# Corn Muffins

**1 cup all-purpose flour**
**¼ cup sugar**
**1 teaspoon salt**
**¾ cup corn meal**
**1 tablespoon baking powder**
**1 egg**
**¼ cup vegetable oil**
**1 cup milk**
**2 tablespoons melted butter**
**3 tablespoons sugar**
**½ teaspoon cinnamon**

Place metal blade in food processor. Add all except last three ingredients to processor. Pulse on and off 3 to 5 seconds or just until blended. Do not overprocess. Scrape down sides of bowl with spatula.

Spoon mixture into 12 greased, medium-sized (2¾-inch diameter) muffin cups. Fill ⅔ full. Bake in preheated 425-degree oven for 12 to 18 minutes, or until edges begin to brown and toothpick inserted in center comes out clean. Combine sugar and cinnamon. Dip tops of hot muffins into melted butter and then into cinnamon-sugar mixture.

**Yield:** 12 muffins

# Cranberry-Apple Muffins

**1 apple, peeled, cored, and cut in quarters**
**1 cup fresh, or unthawed frozen, whole cranberries**
**1 cup sugar**
**1 egg**
**1 cup milk**
**¼ cup vegetable oil**
**2 cups all-purpose flour**
**1 tablespoon baking powder**
**½ teaspoon salt**

Place metal blade in food processor. Add apple, cranberries, and sugar. Pulse on and off for 3 to 5 seconds or until apples and cranberries are diced. Do not overprocess. Add egg, milk, and oil to processor. Pulse on and off once or twice, or just until ingredients are blended. Combine flour, baking powder, and salt. Add to processor. Pulse on and off once or twice, just until blended. Do not overprocess. Scrape down sides of bowl with spatula.

Spoon mixture into 12 greased medium-sized (2¾-inch diameter) muffin cups. Fill ⅔ full. Bake in preheated 400-degree oven for 20 minutes, or until toothpick inserted in center comes out clean.

**Yield:** 12 muffins

# Pumpkin Pear Bread

**1 pear, peeled, cored, and cut in quarters**
**½ cup walnuts**
**1 cup sugar**
**2 eggs**
**½ cup canned cooked pumpkin**
**⅓ cup vegetable oil**
**1¾ cup all-purpose flour**
**1 teaspoon baking soda**
**¾ teaspoon salt**
**½ teaspoon cinnamon**
**¼ teaspoon ground ginger**

Place metal blade in food processor. Add pear, walnuts, and sugar to processor. Pulse on and off for about 5 seconds, or until pears and nuts are diced. Add eggs, pumpkin, and oil, and process for 5 seconds or until ingredients are blended. Combine flour, baking soda, salt, cinnamon, and ginger. Add to pumpkin mixture and pulse on and off for 5 seconds or just until combined.

Spoon batter into a well-greased and floured 8½×4½× 2½-inch loaf pan. Bake in preheated 350-degree oven for 55 to 65 minutes, or until toothpick inserted in center comes out clean.

**Yield:** 1 loaf

# Mushroom and Onion Quiche

**12 mushrooms**
**3 sprigs parsley**
**1 medium onion, peeled**
**3 tablespoons butter**
**3 eggs**
**1 cup light sweet cream**
**4 ounces imported Swiss cheese from Switzerland, cubed**
**½ teaspoon salt**
**¼ teaspoon white pepper**
**1 nine-inch unsweetened Pâté Brisée shell, partially baked* (see page 201)**

Place metal blade in food processor. Add mushrooms, parsley, and onion to processor and chop. Heat butter in a skillet and sauté vegetables from processor until onions are lightly browned and mushrooms are cooked.

Place all remaining ingredients in processor, except Pâté Brisée shell, and pulse on and off until thoroughly blended. Combine with mushroom-onion mixture and pour into partially baked, unsweetened Pâté Brisée shell. Place in preheated 375-degree oven for 35 to 40 minutes or until puffy and nicely browned. A knife inserted 1 inch from center should come out clean. Allow to cool for 10 minutes before serving.

**Serves:** 6

*To partially bake Pâté Brisée shell: Roll out dough and fit into a 9-inch pie plate or quiche pan. Flute edges. Prick bottom of shell with a fork, and bake in a preheated 425-degree oven for 8 to 10 minutes. Cool before filling.

# Cheese and Onion Quiche

**1 nine-inch unbaked pastry shell (see page 201 for Pâté Brisée I recipe)**
**3 eggs, lightly beaten**
**4 ounces Swiss cheese, cut into cubes or strips**
**4 ounces Gruyère cheese, cut into cubes or strips**
**1 tablespoon all-purpose flour**
**1 large onion, peeled**
**½ cup milk**
**½ cup light sweet cream**
**Salt and freshly ground white pepper to taste**
**¼ teaspoon nutmeg**

Brush unbaked pastry shell with a little of the beaten eggs and chill.

Place shredder in food processor and grate cheeses. Pour grated cheese into a bowl and stir in flour. Spoon cheese-flour combination into pastry shell. Place slicer in processor and slice onion thinly and place onion slices on top of grated cheese mixture in pastry shell.

Scald the milk and the cream, remove from heat, and add eggs, stirring for 30 seconds until blended. Season and pour over cheese and onion.

Bake in a preheated 425-degree oven for about 35 minutes or until knife inserted near the center comes out clean.

**Serves:** 6

# Crab Meat Quiche

**1 nine-inch unbaked pastry shell (see page 201 for Pâté Brisée I recipe)**
**4 eggs, lightly beaten**
**1 stalk celery, cut in half**
**3 sprigs parsley**
**3 scallions, each cut in half**
**1½ cups cooked crab meat, picked over and cartilage removed**
**2 tablespoons dry sherry**
**2 cups light sweet cream**
**Salt and freshly ground white pepper to taste**
**¼ teaspoon nutmeg**

Brush unbaked pastry shell with a little of the beaten eggs and chill.

Place metal blade in processor. Add celery, parsley, and scallions to processor and chop finely. Combine in a bowl with crab meat and sherry and spoon vegetable-crab meat mixture into pastry shell.

Scald cream, remove from heat, and add eggs, stirring for 30 seconds until blended. Season and pour over vegetable-crab meat mixture.

Bake in a preheated 425-degree oven for about 35 minutes or until knife inserted near the center comes out clean.

**Serves:** 6

# Bread and Pastry Recipes for Large-Capacity Processors

*When the first edition of this book was published, there was a special section of recipes for machines equipped with dough hooks because only they could knead the heavy doughs, or the large amounts, called for in some bread and pastry recipes.*

*As marvelous as those first processors were, the new ones are even more remarkable, and today's large-capacity processors can turn out fragrant loaves of bread and rich coffee cakes as easily as the machines that come equipped with dough hooks. In addition, Cuisinart offers a plastic, optional dough kneading blade which it recommends for kneading large quantities of yeast dough.*

*The choices are many, and all yours:*

*The recipes in this section can be prepared in a large-capacity food processor (i.e., a machine that has a work bowl with a capacity of approximately 6 to 9 cups). They can also be prepared in a machine with a dough hook, as well as in an older food processor with a smaller capacity (i.e., a machine that has a work bowl with a capacity of approximately 4 to 6 cups).*

*If you're using a smaller processor, the recipes in this section can be adapted by dividing the ingredients in half. Because in some cases that kind of division may seem puzzling, consult the following table when adapting the recipes in this section for the older, or smaller, food processor.*

| LARGE-CAPACITY PROCESSOR | SMALL-CAPACITY PROCESSOR |
| --- | --- |
| **If a recipe calls for:** | **Adapt recipe by using:** |
| 3 tablespoons | 1 tablespoon plus 1½ teaspoons |
| ¼ cup | 2 tablespoons |
| ⅓ cup | 2 tablespoons plus 2 teaspoons |
| ½ cup | 4 tablespoons, or ¼ cup |
| ¾ cup | 6 tablespoons |
| 1½ cups | ¾ cup |
| 5 eggs | 3 eggs |
| 3 eggs | 2 eggs |
| 1 package (¼ ounce) yeast | 2 teaspoons yeast |
| 3 packages (¼ ounce each) yeast | 1 package plus 2 teaspoons yeast |

# Brioches

**⅓ cup warm milk (105 to 115 degrees)**
**2 quarter-ounce packages active dry yeast**
**¼ teaspoon sugar**
**4 to 5 cups all-purpose flour**
**¼ cup sugar**
**1 teaspoon salt**
**5 eggs, beaten**
**½ pound butter, cut in pieces**
**1 egg beaten with 1 tablespoon milk**

Place plastic dough kneading or metal blade in food processor. Add warm milk to processor and sprinkle yeast and sugar over milk. Allow to stand for 5 minutes. Add 3 cups flour, sugar, salt, eggs, and butter to processor. Pulse on and off for 10 seconds, or until all ingredients are thoroughly blended. Add remaining flour, ½ cup at a time, to processor, pulsing on and off until dough begins to form a ball. Dough will be soft. Using spatula, remove dough to a lightly floured board. Knead in just enough flour so that dough is smooth and elastic, and dough bounces back when touched. Place dough in a well-greased bowl, cover, and allow to rise in a warm, draft-free place for 2 to 2½ hours or until doubled in bulk.

Shape three-quarters of the dough into 24 2-inch balls. Place in greased brioche tins or muffin tins. Form remaining dough into 24 small ovals about ½ to ¾ inch in diameter. Make a depression in the center of each large ball. Fit small ovals into depression. Brush top of each brioche with egg-milk mixture. Cover and allow brioches to rise in a warm, draft-free place for about 1 hour or until dough has risen to the top of each tin. Bake in preheated 400-degree oven for 12 to 15 minutes or until golden brown.

**Yield:** 18 to 24 brioches

# Easy Sour Cream Rolls

**1¼ cups warm water (105 to 115 degrees)**
**¼ teaspoon sugar**
**2 quarter-ounce packages active dry yeast**
**⅛ pound butter, cut in pieces**
**¾ cup sour cream**
**1 teaspoon salt**
**2 teaspoons dill weed**
**1 tablespoon grated Parmesan cheese**
**⅓ cup nonfat dry milk solids**
**4 to 5½ cups all-purpose flour**
**½ cup melted butter**

Place plastic dough kneading or metal blade in food processor. Add warm water to processor, and sprinkle sugar and yeast over water. Allow to stand for 5 minutes. Add butter, sour cream, salt, dill weed, cheese, milk solids, and 4 cups flour to processor. Pulse on and off for 10 seconds, or until all ingredients are thoroughly blended. Add remaining flour, ½ cup at a time, to processor, pulsing on and off, until dough begins to form a ball. Dough will be soft. Using a spatula, remove dough to a lightly floured board. Knead in just enough flour so that dough is smooth and elastic and bounces back when touched.

Form dough into 2-inch balls and place in greased muffin tins. Cover and let rise in a warm, draft-free place for about 1½ hours or until dough has about doubled in bulk. Brush tops with melted butter and bake in a preheated 375-degree oven for 30 minutes or until rolls are well browned.

**Yield:** 24 rolls

# Cheddar Cheese Bread

**3 ounces Cheddar cheese**
**2¼ cups warm water (105 to 115 degrees)**
**¼ teaspoon sugar**
**2 quarter-ounce packages active dry yeast**
**⅛ pound butter**
**2 tablespoons grated Parmesan cheese**
**2 tablespoons chives**
**¾ cup nonfat dry milk solids**
**5½ to 6½ cups all-purpose flour**
**¼ cup melted butter**
**Poppy seeds or sesame seeds**

Place shredding disc in food processor. Grate cheese. Remove blade and cheese from processor. Place plastic dough kneading or metal blade in food processor. Add warm water to processor, and sprinkle sugar and yeast over water. Allow to stand for 5 minutes. Add butter, cheeses, chives, dry milk solids, and 3 cups flour to processor. Pulse on and off for 10 seconds, or until all ingredients are thoroughly blended. Add remaining flour, ½ cup at a time, to processor, pulsing on and off until dough begins to form a ball. Dough will be soft. Using spatula, remove dough to a lightly floured board. Knead in just enough flour so that dough is smooth and elastic and bounces back when touched. Divide dough in half. Roll dough out on a floured board into two 14×7-inch rectangles.

Roll each rectangle tightly, jelly-roll style, beginning with the small side. Seal edges and tuck in ends. Place seam side down in two well-greased 9×5×3-inch pans. Brush tops of loaves with melted butter and sprinkle with poppy seeds or sesame seeds. Cover and let rise in a warm, draft-free place for 1½ hours or until doubled in bulk. Bake in a preheated 375-degree oven for 45 minutes or until well browned.

**Yield:** 2 loaves

# Oatmeal Raisin Bread

**2 cups oatmeal**
**½ cup dark molasses**
**½ cup orange juice**
**½ cup raisins**
**⅓ cup vegetable oil**
**1 tablespoon salt**
**2 cups boiling water**
**1 quarter-ounce package active dry yeast**
**½ cup warm water (105 to 115 degrees)**
**6 to 6½ cups all-purpose flour**
**1 egg, beaten with 1 tablespoon milk**

Place plastic dough kneading or metal blade in food processor. Add oatmeal, molasses, orange juice, raisins, vegetable oil, salt, and boiling water to processor. Allow oats to soften 10 minutes. Dissolve yeast in warm water, add to cooled oatmeal mixture, and allow to soften for additional 5 minutes. Add 3 cups flour to processor. Pulse on and off for 10 seconds, or until all ingredients are thoroughly blended. Add remaining flour, ½ cup at a time, to processor, pulsing on and off, until dough begins to form a ball. Dough will be soft. Using a spatula, remove dough to a lightly floured board. Knead in just enough flour so that dough is smooth and elastic and bounces back when touched. Place dough in a greased bowl. Cover and let rise in a warm, draft-free place for about 1½ to 2 hours or until dough has doubled in bulk.

Place dough on a floured board. Divide dough into 3 portions and form into round or oval loaves. Brush tops of loaves with egg-milk mixture. Cover and let rise again until dough has risen by half, about 1½ hours. Bake in a preheated 350-degree oven for 35 to 40 minutes or until golden brown.

**Yield:** 3 loaves

# Rye Bread

**2 cups rye flour**
**¼ cup dark molasses or honey**
**⅓ cup vegetable oil**
**2 teaspoons salt**
**2 cups boiling water**
**2 quarter-ounce packages active dry yeast**
**2 teaspoons caraway seeds**
**6 to 6½ cups all-purpose flour**
**1 egg, beaten with 1 tablespoon milk**

Place plastic dough kneading or metal blade in food processor. Place rye flour, molasses, vegetable oil, salt, and boiling water in processor. Pulse on and off until just combined. Cool to lukewarm for about 8 minutes. Sprinkle yeast over cooled rye mixture and allow to soften for 5 minutes. Add caraway seeds and 3 cups of flour to processor and pulse on and off for 10 seconds, or until blended. Add remaining flour, ½ cup at a time, pulsing on and off, until dough begins to form a ball, about 30 seconds. Dough will be soft. Using a spatula, remove dough to a lightly floured board. Knead in just enough flour so that dough is smooth and elastic and bounces back when touched. Place dough in a well-greased bowl, cover, and allow to rise in a warm, draft-free place for 1½ hours, or until dough has doubled in bulk.

Punch dough down and form into a ball. Place dough on a floured board and divide into 3 equal portions. Form into three oval loaves. Brush tops of loaves with egg-milk mixture. Cover and allow to rise again in a warm, draft-free place, for about 30 minutes, or until dough has risen by half. Bake in a preheated 350-degree oven for 35 to 40 minutes, or until well browned.

**Yield:** 3 loaves

# Whole Wheat Braid Bread

**1¼ cups warm water (105 to 115 degrees)**
**1 quarter-ounce package active dry yeast**
**¼ teaspoon sugar**
**¼ pound butter, cut into pieces**
**¼ cup honey**
**2 eggs**
**2 teaspoons salt**
**⅓ cup nonfat dry milk solids**
**4 cups all-purpose flour**
**2 cups whole wheat flour**
**1 egg beaten with 1 tablespoon milk**
**Sesame seeds or poppy seeds**

Place plastic dough kneading or metal blade in food processor. Add warm water to processor, and sprinkle yeast and sugar over water. Allow to stand for 5 minutes. Add butter, honey, eggs, salt, and nonfat dry milk solids to processor. Pulse on and off for 10 seconds, or until all ingredients are thoroughly blended.

Combine flours and add 4 cups to processor. Pulse on and off for 10 seconds, or until flour is blended. Add remaining flour, ½ cup at a time, to processor, pulsing on and off, until dough begins to form a ball. Dough will be soft.

Using spatula, remove dough to a lightly floured board. Knead in just enough flour so that dough is smooth and elastic and bounces back when touched. Place dough in a lightly greased bowl. Cover and allow to rise in a warm, draft-free place for about 2 hours or until dough has doubled in bulk.

On a board, divide risen dough into 6 equal pieces. Allow dough to rest for about 10 minutes. Roll each piece into an 18 × 1-inch strand. Lay three strands of dough side by side on the board and start to braid the dough from the center toward the ends. Tuck ends under. Place each braided loaf on a baking sheet. Brush the top of each loaf with egg-milk combination and sprinkle with sesame or poppy seeds. Cover and allow to rise in a warm place for 1 hour, or until size has increased by half. Bake in a preheated 375-degree oven for 45 minutes or until loaves are well browned.

**Yield:** 2 loaves

# Honey White Bread

**1 cup warm water (105 to 115 degrees)**
**¼ teaspoon sugar**
**2 quarter-ounce packages active dry yeast**
**1½ cups warm milk (105 to 115 degrees)**
**2 tablespoons honey**
**2 teaspoons salt**
**⅓ cup vegetable oil**
**6 to 7 cups all-purpose flour**

Place plastic dough kneading or metal blade in food processor. Add warm water to processor and sprinkle sugar and yeast over water. Allow to stand for 5 minutes. Add milk, honey, salt, vegetable oil, and 4 cups flour to processor. Pulse on and off for 10 seconds, or until all ingredients are thoroughly blended.

Add remaining flour, ½ cup at a time, to processor, pulsing on and off, until dough begins to form a ball. Dough will be soft. Using spatula, remove dough to a lightly floured board.

Knead in just enough flour so that dough is smooth and elastic and bounces back when touched. Shape dough into 2 balls. Let stand for 10 minutes.

Roll each ball of dough into an oval. Fold each oval in half lengthwise. Pinch the seams to seal, and tuck the ends under. Place seam side down in 2 well-greased 9×5×3-inch pans. Cover and let rise in a warm, draft-free place for 1 to 1½ hours or until doubled in bulk. Bake in a preheated 350-degree oven for approximately 45 minutes or until well browned.

**Yield:** 2 loaves

# Pizza

**1 pound mozzarella cheese**
**1 small wedge (approximately ⅛ pound) Parmesan cheese**
**3 green peppers, cored and seeded**
**1 medium onion, peeled**
**½ pound mushrooms**
**1¼ cups warm water (105 to 115 degrees)**
**¼ teaspoon sugar**
**3 quarter-ounce packages active dry yeast**
**5 to 6 cups all-purpose flour**
**2 teaspoons salt**
**¼ teaspoon pepper**
**¾ teaspoon dry basil**
**3 cups tomato sauce**
**2 teaspoons dry oregano**
**½ teaspoon garlic salt**

Place shredder in food processor. Grate cheeses. Remove shredder. Remove cheese from processor and reserve. Place slicer in food processor. Individually slice peppers, onion, and mushrooms. Remove slicer. Remove vegetables from processor and reserve.

Place plastic dough kneading or metal blade in food processor. Add warm water to processor bowl and sprinkle sugar and yeast over water. Allow to stand for 5 minutes. Add 3 cups flour, salt, pepper, and basil to processor. Pulse on and off for 10 seconds, or until all ingredients are thoroughly blended. Add remaining flour, ½ cup at a time, to processor, pulsing on and off, until dough begins to form a ball. Dough will be soft. Using a spatula, remove dough to a lightly floured board. Knead in just enough flour so that dough is smooth and elastic and bounces back when touched. Place dough in a floured bowl. Cover and allow to rise in a warm, draft-free place for 2 to 3 hours, or until dough has doubled in bulk.

Stretch dough to fit two cookie sheets, or two 12-inch round pans. Cover pizza dough with tomato sauce and grated cheeses. Sprinkle with oregano and garlic salt. Top with sliced vegetables. Bake pizza in a preheated 450-degree oven for 20 minutes, or until crust is brown, sauce hot, and cheese melted.

**Serves:** 8 to 10

# Apricot Pecan Coffee Ring

**DOUGH**

**1½ cups milk**
**½ cup sugar**
**¼ pound butter**
**1 teaspoon salt**
**2 quarter-ounce packages active dry yeast**
**5 to 6 cups all-purpose flour**
**3 eggs**
**1 egg, beaten with 1 tablespoon milk**

**FILLING**

**2 jars (12 ounces each) apricot preserves and 1½ cups chopped pecans, mixed together**

*To Make Dough:*

In a small saucepan, heat milk, sugar, butter, and salt to 115 degrees. Butter does not have to be completely melted.

Place plastic dough kneading or metal blade in food processor. Add warm milk-sugar mixture to processor and sprinkle yeast over milk. Allow to stand for 5 minutes.

Add 4 cups flour and eggs to processor and pulse on and off for 10 seconds, or until thoroughly blended. Add remaining flour ½ cup at a time, pulsing on and off until dough begins to form a ball. Dough will be soft.

Using a spatula, remove dough to a lightly floured board. Knead in just enough flour so that dough is smooth and elastic and bounces back when touched. Place dough in a well-greased bowl, cover, and allow to rise in a warm, draft-free place for 1½ hours or until dough has doubled in bulk.

Divide dough in half. Roll each half into an 18×12-inch rectangle. Place half of filling mixture in the center of each rectangle, spreading filling down the length of each strip to within 1 inch of ends. Roll each rectangle of dough tightly, jelly-roll style, starting with the long side. Seal well. Form each rectangle of rolled dough into a ring and make slits in the dough 2 inches apart and 1 inch deep. Press to flatten.

Place pastry rings on a cookie sheet, cover, and allow to rise in a warm, draft-free place for about 1 hour or until dough has doubled in bulk. Brush with egg-milk mixture. Bake in a preheated 350-degree oven for 45 minutes or until well browned. Serve warm, or allow cake to cool, and sprinkle with powdered, or confectioner's, sugar.

**Yield:** 2 coffee cakes

# Swedish Tea Ring

**DOUGH**

**¼ cup warm water (105 to 115 degrees)**
**¼ teaspoon sugar**
**1 quarter-ounce package active dry yeast**
**¾ cup warm milk (105 to 115 degrees)**
**¼ cup melted butter**
**1 egg**
**3 to 3¾ cups all-purpose flour**
**1 teaspoon salt**
**¼ cup sugar**

**FILLING**

**½ cup sugar**
**2 teaspoons cinnamon**
**½ cup melted butter**
**½ cup raisins**
**¼ cup maraschino cherries, coarsely chopped**
**¼ cup walnuts, coarsely chopped**

*To Make Dough:*

Place plastic dough kneading or metal blade in food processor. Add warm water to processor, and sprinkle sugar and yeast over water. Allow to stand for 5 minutes.

Add milk, butter, egg, 2½ cups flour, salt, and sugar to processor. Pulse on and off for 10 seconds, or until all ingredients are thoroughly blended. Add remaining flour, ½ cup at a time, to processor, pulsing on and off until dough begins to form a ball. Dough will be soft.

Using spatula, remove dough to a lightly floured board and knead in just enough flour so that dough is smooth and elastic and bounces back when touched. Remove dough and place in a well-greased bowl. Cover and set in a warm, draft-free place for 1½ hours. Punch down, cover, and let rise again for 30 minutes. Punch down again.

*To Assemble Tea Ring:*

On a floured board, roll dough into a rectangle 14 inches long and 10 inches wide. Combine sugar and cinnamon. Brush top of rectangle with melted butter and sprinkle sugar-cinnamon mixture over dough. Distribute raisins, cherries, and walnuts over dough. Roll dough up tightly from wide end. Seal seam securely. Form a ring and seal ends together. Cut ⅔ of the way through the ring at 1-inch intervals. Twist sections on the side. Let dough rise for 20 to 30 minutes. Bake in a preheated 325-degree oven for 25 to 35 minutes or until top is golden brown. If you should wish to glaze this tea ring, combine ½ cup powdered sugar with 1 tablespoonful of warm water and drizzle over cooled tea ring.

**Yield:** 1 large tea ring

Homemade pasta? Yes! And once you taste it, you'll have a hard time going back to the store-bought variety. Pasta dough is prepared in the food processor and then rolled out and cut by hand. If you have a pasta-cutting machine that cuts pasta into various widths, that provides another short-cut to pasta making.

There's a tremendous variety of dishes that can be made with pasta, and freshly made noodles extend meals wonderfully. Chopped meat goes a lot further in a spaghetti sauce than in a hamburger, and the end result is so flavorful that no one will remember the money saved—they'll be too busy talking about the wonderful taste!

When making a large batch of pasta, allow the cut noodles to dry completely and store in a dry place, and they will keep for months or even longer. (There will be such a demand for your pasta dishes, however, that storage may never be a problem.)

# Cannelloni

**PASTA**

**2¼ cups all-purpose flour**
**3 eggs**
**¼ cup water**
**1 tablespoon oil**

**MEAT FILLING**

**¾ pound beef, trimmed and cut into cubes**
**¾ pound veal, trimmed and cut into cubes**
**1 chicken breast, boned, skinned, and cut into cubes**
**1 clove garlic, peeled**
**1 small onion, peeled**
**3 sprigs parsley**
**1 medium carrot, cleaned, scraped, and cut into 4 pieces**
**2 slices white bread, crusts trimmed, broken into large pieces**
**2 eggs**

*To Make Pasta Dough:*

Place metal blade in food processor. Add all ingredients for pasta to processor and pulse on and off until dough forms a ball. Remove from processor and refrigerate for 30 minutes.

*To Make Meat Filling:*

Place meat in food processor and chop until meat has the consistency of hamburger. Depending on the size of your processor, you may have to do this in two steps. Add all other ingredients to processor and pulse on and off until all ingredients are chopped and thoroughly combined. Spoon meat mixture into a bowl and reserve.

Roll out dough on a well-floured board, as thinly as possible. Cut dough into 4-inch squares. Cook squares (about 12 at a time) in 6 quarts of rapidly boiling salted water for about 6 minutes. Dough squares should be *al dente*—slightly firm, not mushy. Remove dough squares from boiling water with a slotted spoon and drain, until all dough squares are cooked and drained.

Spoon about 3 tablespoons of meat filling onto each cooked square. Spread mixture on square, then roll the filled Cannelloni square up and place seam side down in a large buttered baking dish. When all the Cannelloni squares are in the baking dish, top evenly, first with Béchamel Sauce (page 139) and then with Italian-Style Tomato Sauce (page 74).

Bake in preheated 350-degree oven for 25 minutes or until sauce is bubbling.

**Serves:** 6 to 8

# Fettuccine Primavera

**FETTUCCINE**

**2 cups all-purpose flour**
**2 egg yolks**
**1 egg**
**2 teaspoons salt**
**⅛ to ¼ cup water**
**¼ pound butter, melted**

**SAUCE**

**2 medium zucchini, washed and scraped**
**½ pound mushrooms, washed**
**4 tablespoons butter**
**1 cup heavy cream**
**4 tablespoons grated Parmesan cheese**

*To Make Fettuccine:*

Place metal blade in food processor. Add flour, egg yolks, egg, and salt to processor. Pulse on and off once or twice, or until just combined. With the machine running, gradually add water. Continue processing only until mixture begins to form a ball. Using spatula, remove dough to a lightly floured board. Knead in just enough additional flour until dough is smooth and elastic. Cover and let rest 10 minutes.

Divide dough into 4 equal parts. Roll each piece of dough on a floured board. Dough must be rolled paper-thin. After dough is flattened, remove from board and gently stretch with your hands until light can be seen through the sheet of dough. Cut dough into ¼-inch strips. Place strips on clean dry towel. Allow to dry for about 2 hours.

When noodles have dried somewhat, cook in boiling, salted water. Freshly made noodles cook much more quickly than the store-bought kind. Fettuccine noodles will be cooked in approximately 5 to 7 minutes and are best when cooked *al dente,* or slightly firm to the bite. Drain cooked noodles and toss in melted butter.

*To Make Sauce:*

Place slicing disc in food processor. Slice zucchini and mushrooms. Heat butter in a large skillet. Sauté zucchini and mushrooms over medium-high heat, stirring. Vegetables should not be overcooked, and they should be cooked sufficiently in 5 to 10 minutes. Spoon vegetables, butter, and juices from skillet over cooked fettuccine. Add in cream and grated cheese. Heat, tossing gently, until noodles are coated with cream and all ingredients are thoroughly hot.

**Serves:** 4

# Gnocchi

**1 pound medium potatoes, peeled, cut into cubes, boiled, and drained**
**2 tablespoons light sweet cream**
**2 tablespoons butter**
**2 teaspoons chives**
**3 sprigs parsley**
**½ cup water**
**3 tablespoons butter**
**½ teaspoon salt**
**1 cup all-purpose flour**

Place metal blade in food processor. Add potatoes, cream, butter, chives, and parsley to processor and pulse on and off until ingredients are thoroughly combined.

Combine water, butter, and salt in a saucepan and bring to a boil. Stir ½ cup of flour into water all at once until mixture is combined. Heat water-flour mixture over medium-low heat for 2 to 3 minutes. Add this flour-paste mixture to ingredients in processor and pulse on and off. Scrape down sides of bowl with a spatula. Mixture will be sticky and heavy. Spoon mixture into a floured bowl and refrigerate for 3 to 4 hours.

Turn gnocchi dough out onto a well-floured board and knead in remaining ½ cup of flour. At this point you should be able to work dough with your hands. If mixture seems too sticky, add more flour, a little at a time.

Divide dough into 8 or 10 pieces. Roll each piece into a long strand that is about ½-inch thick. Cut each strand of dough into 2-inch pieces.

Cook gnocchi in boiling salted water for 2 to 3 minutes, or until gnocchi rise to the top of the water. Drain gnocchi, and toss with butter, heavy cream and grated Parmesan cheese, or serve with your favorite spaghetti sauce.

**Serves:** 6 to 8

# Spinach Noodles

**½ pound fresh spinach, washed, or half of a 10-ounce package frozen spinach, thawed**
**2 eggs**
**2 cups all-purpose flour**
**1 teaspoon salt**
**¼ teaspoon freshly ground pepper**

Cook spinach in a small amount of boiling salted water for 3 minutes. Drain well, pressing out as much water as possible. Cool. Place metal blade in food processor. Add spinach, eggs, flour, salt, and pepper. Pulse on and off once or twice or until just combined. With the machine running, gradually add water until mixture begins to form a ball. Using spatula, remove dough to a lightly floured board. Knead in just enough additional flour until dough is smooth and elastic. Cover and let rest 10 minutes.

Divide dough into 4 equal parts. Roll each piece of dough on a floured board. Dough must be rolled paper thin. After dough is flattened, remove from board and gently stretch with your hands until light can be seen through the sheet of dough. Cut dough in ¼-inch strips. Place strips on clean dry towel. Allow to dry for about 2 hours.

When noodles have dried somewhat, cook in boiling salted water. Freshly made noodles cook much more quickly than the store-bought kind. Noodles will be cooked in approximately 5 to 7 minutes and are best when cooked *al dente,* or slightly firm.

Serve spinach noodles with your favorite spaghetti sauce, or combine with fettuccine noodles and serve with butter, heavy cream, and grated Parmesan cheese. When fettuccine and spinach noodles are combined in this manner, the dish is called *paglia e fieno,* meaning hay and straw, and is one of the delights of Northern Italian cuisine.

**Serves:** 4

# Hungarian *Nockerle* Dumplings

**2 eggs**
**2 cups all-purpose flour**
**1 teaspoon salt**
**½ to 1 cup water**

Place metal blade in food processor. Add eggs, flour, and salt. With the machine running, gradually add water to the processor. Continue processing until mixture forms a ball. Use only enough water to form a ball. Mixture should not be dry but semisoft.

Cook dumplings in a large pot of boiling, salted water. Using a tablespoon, cut off approximately half a tablespoon of dumpling mixture and drop into boiling water. After all the dumplings are in the boiling water, cook for 20 minutes. Drain and rinse with cold water. Serve with Chicken Paprikas, goulash, or your favorite stew.

**Serves:** 4

# BABY FOOD

Thanks to the magical, wonderful food processor, you can now prepare healthful meals for your baby easily and inexpensively. And since you'll be preparing the foods yourself, you can be sure that your baby won't be eating unnecessary sugar, salt, preservatives, additives, or food coloring.

If you wish, you can adapt your own dinners to your baby's meals, and you'll be surprised to learn that a baby's tastes can be pretty sophisticated. One eight-month-old loved scallops that had been cooked with garlic and which his mother pureed for him in the food processor.

The recipes in this section can be prepared by pureeing, chopping, or dicing—depending on the age of your baby. If you wish, prepare a larger amount and freeze the leftovers for later use. One clever method is to spoon the processed food into an ice cube tray, leaving the ice cube divider in place. After the food is frozen, you can remove a cube at a time and heat before serving. Or, if you prefer, remove all the cubes, wrap separately, label each one, and you'll have a freezer full of meals ready to serve to your baby.

Of course, it's important to consult your pediatrician when determining your baby's diet. Some doctors recommend only formula, cereal, and bananas for infants, but if your doctor advises solid food, you'll find a nutritional variety of easy-to-prepare recipes in this section.

By the way, it is easy to adapt any of these recipes for babies of any age simply by adjusting the consistency of the mixture. To prepare strained baby food for infants aged three to eight months, puree the ingredients. For junior baby food for infants aged eight months to one year, finely chop the ingredients. For baby food for toddlers one year to eighteen months, dice.

# Basic Breakfast: Cereal and Fruit

**¼ cup baby cereal (any variety)**
**½ cup warm milk or formula**
**½ cup fruit, canned or fresh**

Place metal blade in food processor. Add all ingredients and process until desired consistency is reached.

**Yield:** 1 cup

# Cereal, Egg Yolk, and Bacon

**¼ cup rice cereal**
**½ cup warm milk or formula**
**1 egg yolk**
**1 slice bacon, cooked and cut into 1-inch pieces**

Place metal blade in food processor. Add all ingredients and process until desired consistency is reached.

**Yield:** ½ cup

# Basic Dinner

*You can use portions of your own dinner to prepare the following recipe.*

**½ cup cooked meat (or fish or poultry)**
**¼ cup boiled, diced potato (or ¼ cup cooked rice or noodles)**
**¼ cup cooked vegetable**
**¼ to ½ cup milk (or broth or water)**

Place metal blade in food processor. Add meat and process until finely chopped. Add potato, vegetable and milk and process until desired consistency is reached. Heat before serving if desired.

**Yield:** ¾ cup

# Sunday Chicken Dinner

**½ cup cubed cooked chicken, skin removed**
**¼ cup cooked carrots.**
**2 tablespoons cooked, diced potatoes**
**¼ cup warm milk**

Place metal blade in food processor. Add chicken and process until finely chopped. Add carrots, potatoes, and milk and process until desired consistency is reached. Heat before serving if desired.

**Yield:** ¾ cup

# David Elliot's Seafood Dinner

**½ cup cooked whitefish fillet (or scallops)**
**¼ cup cooked rice (or potatoes)**
**¼ cup warm milk (or broth)**

Place metal blade in food processor. Add all ingredients and process until desired consistency is reached. Heat before serving if desired.

**Yield:** ¾ cup

# Steak and Potato Dinner

**½ cup cooked steak (or roast beef or hamburger), cut in small cubes**
**½ small baked potato**
**¼ cup warm milk**
**1 teaspoon butter**

Place metal blade in food processor. Add steak and process until finely chopped. Add potato, milk, and butter and process until desired consistency is reached. Heat before serving if desired.

**Yield:** ¾ cup

# Meatballs and Spaghetti

**½ cup cooked macaroni or spaghetti**
**¼ cup tomato sauce**
**1 small meatball**

Place metal blade in food processor. Add all ingredients and process until desired consistency is reached. Heat before serving if desired.

**Yield:** 1 cup

# Vegetable Soup

**½ cup mixed vegetables, cooked**
**¼ cup chicken broth**
**¼ cup cooked pastina**

Place metal blade in food processor. Add vegetables and broth. Process until desired consistency is reached. Stir in cooked pastina. Heat before serving if desired.

**Yield:** ¾ cup

# Apple-Prune Sauce

**1 apple, peeled, cored, cut into chunks**
**4 dried prunes, pitted, cut into quarters**
**⅓ cup apple juice or orange juice**
**¼ cup water**

Place apple chunks, prunes, and fruit juice in a small saucepan. Cover and cook over very low heat for 10 minutes. Place metal blade in food processor. Add cooked fruit and water. Process until desired consistency is reached.

**Yield:** ¾ cup

# Banana and Pear Sauce

**½ cup canned or fresh pear slices**
**½ small banana**
**¼ cup pear liquid or fruit juice**

Place metal blade in food processor. Add all ingredients and process until desired consistency is reached.

**Yield:** ¾ cup

# Pureed Dried Fruits

**½ cup dried apricots, pitted prunes, or mixed fruits**
**¾ to 1 cup water**

Place fruit and water in a small saucepan. Cover and cook over very low heat for 10 minutes. Place metal blade in food processor. Add cooked fruit and water. Process until desired consistency is reached.

**Yield:** 1 cup

# Cottage Cheese and Fruit

**¾ cup cottage cheese**
**½ cup fresh or canned fruit**
**3 tablespoons fruit liquid or juice**

Place metal blade in food processor. Add all ingredients and process until desired consistency is reached.

**Yield:** 1 cup

# JAMS, RELISHES, CHUTNEYS, AND NUT BUTTERS

Your food processor can turn a box of dried apricots into a beautiful smooth puree that's worthy of filling your finest crêpes. It can chop ginger for chutney and fruits for relishes. It can chop nuts into the freshest nut butter you've ever tasted and produce cups of fresh bread crumbs from leftover loaves of French or Italian bread. A pot of homemade Peach Butter on the breakfast table, a cut-glass bowl filled with spicy Indian chutney that you made in the processor; these are small touches that can make a meal an event.

Remember that homemade butters, jams, and preserves contain no preservatives, and cannot be kept as long as commercial products.

# Apricot Jam

*Alice, in Wonderland, complained that it was never jam today. Now, thanks to the processor, it can be jam today—and every day—without too much effort.*

**1 eleven- to twelve-ounce box dried apricots**
**Water**
**1 cup sugar, or more, to taste**

Place apricots in a large saucepan. Cover with water and cook over low heat until apricots are soft enough to be broken up with the back of a spoon. Allow apricots to cool in water. Place metal blade in food processor. Spoon apricots and the water in which they were cooked into processor. Puree until apricots are completely smooth. Depending on the size of your processor bowl, you may have to do this in two steps.

When all the apricots are thoroughly and smoothly pureed, return puree to saucepan, and over very, very low heat, start cooking the jam. Add sugar, half a cup at a time. Stir, taste during cooking, and add more sugar if you wish. Cook uncovered for approximately 1 hour or until jam is thick. Test by putting a teaspoonful of jam on a plate and putting the plate in the refrigerator for 5 minutes. If the cooled puree is thick, you have apricot jam. Store covered in refrigerator or seal in sterilized jars.

This jam is especially delicious as a filling for rolled crêpes.

**Yield:** Approximately 2 pints

# Peachy Butter

**4 pounds ripe peaches (about 20), peeled, halved, and pitted**
**½ cup water**
**2 cups sugar**
**1¼ teaspoons grated lemon rind**
**½ teaspoon cinnamon**
**¼ teaspoon cardamom**

Place peaches in a large saucepan, add water, and cook over low heat until peaches are soft. Place metal blade in food processor. Spoon peaches and all their cooking juice into processor and puree thoroughly. Return peach puree to saucepan and combine with remaining ingredients. Cook over low heat until mixture thickens, about 45 minutes, Stir frequently. Store, covered, in refrigerator or seal in sterilized jars.

**Yield:** 2 pints

# Nectarine 'n' Tomato Jam, Country Style

**1 pound fresh ripe nectarines (about 5 or 6), peeled, pitted, and halved**
**1 pound red ripe tomatoes, peeled and cored**
**¼ cup lemon juice**
**1 teaspoon grated lemon rind**
**¼ teaspoon ground allspice**
**1 one-and-three-quarter-ounce package powdered pectin**
**4 cups sugar**

Place metal blade in food processor. Add nectarines to processor and chop. Remove to a large saucepan. Place tomatoes in food processor and chop. Add to nectarines. Add lemon juice, lemon rind, allspice, and pectin and bring mixture to a hard boil. Stir in sugar and bring to a full, rolling boil. Boil hard for 1 minute. Remove from heat and skim off foam. Store, covered, in refrigerator or seal in sterilized jars.

**Yield:** 5 eight-ounce jars

# Mincemeat and Pear Relish

**2 cups prepared mincemeat**
**½ cup lemon juice**
**1½ teaspoons salt**
**1 teaspoon dry mustard**
**½ teaspoon rosemary**
**Dash of cayenne pepper**
**5 large Bartlett pears, cored and cut into quarters**
**1 small sweet red pepper, cored, seeded, and cut into 4 strips**
**1 small green pepper, cored, seeded, and cut into 4 strips**

Combine mincemeat, lemon juice, salt, mustard, rosemary, and cayenne in large saucepan and heat mixture to boiling point over medium heat.

Place metal blade in food processor. Chop pears and add to mincemeat mixture. Allow to simmer uncovered for 15 minutes. Chop peppers in food processor and add to mincemeat-pear mixture. Cook for an additional 5 minutes. Store covered in refrigerator or seal in sterilized jars.

**Yield:** Approximately 1 quart

# Rajah's Special Chutney

**4 ounces fresh ginger root, pared and cut into chunks**
**1½ cups water**
**½ tablespoon salt**
**3½ cups sugar**
**1¼ cups vinegar**
**¼ cup Worcestershire sauce**
**1 small onion, peeled**
**2 cloves garlic, peeled**
**1 small canned green chili pepper**
**3½ pounds fresh nectarines, halved and pitted**
**1 cup golden seedless raisins**
**½ cup fresh lime juice**

Place metal blade in food processor. Add ginger to processor and chop until fine. Place ginger in saucepan with water and salt, and simmer about 20 minutes or until ginger is almost tender. Drain ginger, reserving ¼ cup liquid. Mix this ginger liquid with sugar, vinegar, and Worcestershire sauce.

Place onion in food processor and, with machine on, drop garlic through feed tube into processor. Chop and add to ginger liquid. Bring mixture to a boil. Chop chili pepper and add to ginger-liquid mixture. Place slicing disc in food processor and slice nectarines. Add nectarines, cooked ginger root, raisins, and lime juice to ginger-liquid mixture and cook over low-medium heat until mixture thickens, about 1½ hours. Chutney will thicken even more as it chills. Store, covered, in refrigerator, or seal in sterilized jars.

**Yield:** Approximately 8 half-pint jars

# Cranapple Relish

**1 cup shelled walnuts**
**1 cup sugar**
**1 cup fresh, uncooked cranberries**
**2 apples, peeled, cored, and cut into quarters**
**½ cup orange juice**

Place metal blade in food processor. Add all ingredients to processor. Pulse machine on and off for approximately 10 seconds, or until ingredients are coarsely chopped. Spoon relish into a bowl and cover. Chill overnight. Serve with roast turkey or ham.

**Yield:** Approximately 4 cups

# Cashew Butter

**3 cups cashew nuts**
**1 to 2 tablespoons vegetable oil**
**Salt to taste**

Place metal blade in food processor. Add cashews to processor and process until nuts form a ball. This will take about 3 minutes. Continue processing, and nut ball will turn into paste. Scrape down sides of bowl, add oil gradually, and continue processing until butterlike texture is reached. Add salt to taste.

Homemade nut butters must be kept in the refrigerator as there are no preservatives used.

**Yield:** Approximately 1½ cups

# Peanut Butter

*I recommend that, to make peanut butter, you use fresh-roasted peanuts in the shell. True, you do have to hand-shell them and remove the thin red skin that covers the nut, but the result—a creamy natural peanut butter—is well worth the trouble.*

**3 cups shelled and skinned roasted peanuts**
**Salt to taste**

Place metal blade in food processor. Add nuts to processor and process until peanuts form a ball. This will take about 3 minutes. Continue processing, and peanut ball will turn into a paste. Scrape down sides of bowl and continue processing until butter-like texture is reached. Add salt to taste.

Homemade nut butters must be kept in the refrigerator as there are no preservatives used.

**Yield:** Approximately 1½ cups

*Variation:* For Chunky Style Peanut Butter, add an additional ½ cup peanuts to processor when nut ball begins to turn into paste. Continue processing as before.

# DESSERTS

Desserts: the last course of the meal; the course we waited for so eagerly as children; and the course that is still the favorite. Lavish desserts such as Cream Puffs with Hot Fudge Sauce can now be prepared more easily thanks to the food processor, as can a variety of rich cheesecakes.

The good news for dessert lovers is that there's a new accessory available for one of the processors that can really whip cream and turn egg whites into glossy peaks. But don't despair if your machine doesn't come with such an accessory; most machines can whip cream until it's richly thick, even though it won't be voluminous with extra air. If your machine doesn't come with a special beater, use a small hand beater or a whisk to beat egg whites into a meringue.

If cookies and cakes are your favorites, be careful not to overprocess when preparing them in a food processor. Processors work quickly, and you must move quickly, too, pulsing or turning the machine off before cookie dough and cake batter become too heavy.

Use the recipes in this section as a guide when adapting your own dessert favorites to the food processor.

# Cream Puffs with Hot Fudge Sauce

**PUFF SHELLS (PÂTÉ À CHOUX)**

**1 cup water**
**4 tablespoons butter**
**1 teaspoon sugar**
**½ cup all-purpose flour**
**2 eggs**

**CREAM FILLING**

**2 cups heavy sweet cream**
**1 tablespoon sugar**
**1 teaspoon vanilla**

**HOT FUDGE SAUCE**

**3 one-ounce squares semisweet chocolate**
**1 teaspoon vanilla**
**2 to 3 tablespoons sugar, to taste**
**¼ cup hot milk**

*To Make Puff Shells:*

Heat water and butter in a saucepan to boiling point. Using a wooden spoon, quickly stir in sugar and all the flour. Cook over low heat for about 2 minutes or until mixture coats the bottom of the pan and begins to move away from the sides. Cool slightly.

Place metal blade in food processor. Add pâté à choux mixture to processor. Turn machine on and add eggs, one at a time, pulsing on and off for several seconds or until the puff paste is shiny and smooth. Drop puff paste by the tablespoonful onto a greased cookie sheet. Bake in a preheated 425-degree oven for

20 minutes. Lower temperature of oven to 375 degrees. Make a 1-inch slit in each puff and continue baking for approximately 10 minutes longer or until puffs are nicely browned and crusty. Remove from oven and cool. Cut tops off puffs and scoop out uncooked portion from within each puff.

*To Make Cream Filling:*

Wash processor bowl and metal blade, and dry thoroughly. Place food processor bowl, metal blade, and heavy cream in the freezer. Chill 10 to 15 minutes. Pour chilled cream into cold bowl. Add sugar and vanilla. Process until cream thickens, about 30 to 40 seconds. Do not overprocess or the result will be butter. (If your machine comes with beater accessory, use instead of metal blade.) Fill cooled puffs with cream and cover tops of puffs. Refrigerate.

*To Make Hot Fudge Sauce:*

Wash processor bowl and metal blade once again. Place all ingredients for sauce in food processor and process until ingredients are well blended.

Heat and spoon sauce over puffs, and serve.

**Serves:** 8

# Chocolate Mousse

**1 six-ounce package semisweet chocolate pieces**
**¼ cup, or 5 tablespoons, hot, black, strong coffee**
**2 tablespoons sugar**
**4 egg yolks**
**2 tablespoons dark rum**
**4 egg whites, stiffly beaten**

Place metal blade in food processor. Add chocolate pieces to processor and chop finely, pulsing on and off, and scraping chocolate down from sides of the bowl. Add hot coffee and sugar and process until blended. Add egg yolks and rum gradually and continue processing until mixture is well blended. Pour mixture into a bowl and fold in egg whites. Chill thoroughly before serving.

**Serves:** 8

# Aunt Clara's Chocolate Chip Cake

**¼ pound butter, cut into 6 or 8 pieces**
**1 cup sugar**
**2 eggs**
**½ cup milk**
**½ teaspoon vanilla extract**
**1¾ cups all-purpose flour**
**½ teaspoon salt**
**2 teaspoons baking powder**
**½ cup semisweet chocolate bits**

Place metal blade in food processor. Add butter, sugar, eggs, milk, and vanilla to processor. Process until ingredients are blended. Add flour, salt, and baking powder gradually to food processor. Pulse on and off while processing, and process only as long as it takes flour to disappear into other ingredients. Pour into a buttered 9-inch cake pan and stir in chocolate bits.

Bake for 25 minutes in a preheated 375-degree oven. Allow to cool, and cut into squares before serving.

**Serves:** 6 to 8

# Creamy Pear Ice

**3 large Bartlett pears, each peeled, cored, and cut into 4 pieces**
**½ cup pineapple juice**
**1 cup sugar**
**½ teaspoon salt**
**1 three-ounce package cream cheese, cut into 3 pieces**
**½ cup heavy sweet cream**
**2 tablespoons lemon juice**

Place metal blade in food processor. Place pears and pineapple juice in processor and process until a smooth puree is attained. Add sugar, salt, cream cheese, sweet cream, and lemon juice gradually to processor and continue processing until well blended. Pour into a loaf pan or other container, cover, and freeze overnight.

Several hours before serving, cut Pear Ice into chunks. Place metal blade in food processor. Add Pear Ice to processor, and process until smooth. Spoon Pear Ice into a container, cover, and return to freezer. Freeze again before serving.

**Serves:** 6 to 8

# Strawberry Tarts with Crème Pâtissière

**TART SHELLS**

**1¼ cups all-purpose flour**
**¼ pound chilled butter, cut into 6 or 8 pieces**
**1 tablespoon sugar**
**¼ teaspoon salt**
**1 tablespoon cold water**
**1 egg**

**CRÈME PÂTISSIÈRE**

**⅓ cup sugar**
**3½ tablespoons cornstarch**
**6 lightly beaten egg yolks**
**2 cups milk**
**½ tablespoon vanilla extract**
**2 tablespoons Grand Marnier liqueur**

*To Make Tart Shells:*

Place metal blade in food processor. Add flour, butter, sugar, and salt to processor and process until the mixture has the consistency of coarse meal. With the machine running, add the water and the egg and continue processing until mixture forms a ball. Refrigerate at least 30 minutes before using.

Roll out dough and press into the six individual small tart pans. Prick each shell with a fork at bottom and sides. Trim edges, and flute with your fingers. Place tart shells on a baking sheet and bake in a preheated 400-degree oven for about 10 to 15 minutes or until shells are delicately brown. Cool before filling.

**Yield:** 6 small tart shells

*To Make Crème Pâtissière:*

Combine sugar, cornstarch, and egg yolks in a saucepan. Scald the milk and pour it gradually over egg mixture. Cook over low heat, stirring constantly with a wire whisk or egg beater until mixture is thick and smooth. Keep heat low and do not allow the mixture to come to a boil. After removing from heat, stir in vanilla and Grand Marnier. Cool before filling tart shells. You will have about 3 cups of Crème Pâtissière.

**TOPPING**

**1 cup red currant glaze, prepared by cooking 1 cup of red currant jelly with two tablespoonfuls of sugar, until thick**
**1 pint fresh strawberries, washed and hulled**

*To Assemble Tarts:*

Paint inside of each tart shell with currant glaze and allow to cool for about 5 minutes. Fill each tart shell about ⅔ full with *crème pâtissière*. Arrange fresh strawberries close together around edge of each tart and in center, with points up. Spoon more currant glaze over strawberries and refrigerate tarts until you're ready to serve them.

**Serves:** 6

# Cheesecakes

*Food processors seem to have been designed for the creation of delicate, light cheesecakes. Practically everyone has a favorite cheesecake, and while we can't include recipes for all the variations, we have selected a representative sample, ranging from strawberry and cherry cheesecake to ricotta cheesecake and a Hungarian favorite, pot cheese and fresh dill cheesecake.*

## Cherry Cheese Pie in Graham Cracker Crumb Crust

**CRUST**

**12 graham crackers, broken into large pieces**
**1 tablespoon sugar**
**4 tablespoons butter, melted**

**FILLING**

**2 eight-ounce packages cream cheese, each cut into 4 pieces**
**¾ cup sugar**
**4 eggs**
**1 cup sour cream**
**1 tablespoon all-purpose flour**
**1 teaspoon vanilla**
**2 teaspoons lemon juice**
**¼ cup half-and-half**
**1 one-pound-five-ounce can cherry pie filling**

*To Make Crust:*

Place metal blade in food processor. Add graham cracker pieces to processor and process until you have fine crumbs. Add sugar and continue processing until well mixed. Pour crumb-sugar mixture into a bowl and add butter, mixing until crumbs are moistened. Press crumbs into a 9- or 10-inch buttered pie plate and chill before using.

*To Make Filling:*

For filling, place cream cheese and sugar in food processor, and, using metal blade, blend until creamy. Add all remaining ingredients, except cherry pie filling, and continue processing until smooth.

Pour filling into pie shell and bake in a preheated 350-degree oven for 45 to 55 minutes or until a toothpick inserted an inch from the center comes out dry. Turn oven off and allow pie to cool in oven for 15 to 20 minutes. Top of cheesecake may crack during baking. This will not affect the flavor in any way. Refrigerate for at least 4 hours and then top with cherry pie filling.

**Serves:** 8

# Marble Strawberry Cheesecake

**1 nine-inch unbaked French pastry shell made with sugar (see page 203 for Pâté Brisée Sucrée II recipe)**
**3 eight-ounce packages cream cheese, softened, each package cut into 4 pieces**
**1 cup sugar**
**3 eggs**
**1 cup sour cream**
**2 tablespoons all-purpose flour**
**1 six-ounce package semisweet chocolate pieces, melted**
**1 cup whipped cream**
**2 twelve-ounce packages frozen strawberries, thawed and drained**

Line the bottom and sides of a 9-inch springform pan with Pâté Brisée Sucrée II. Prick dough at the bottom and place in a preheated 425-degree oven for about 10 minutes or until lightly browned. Set aside and allow to cool.

Place metal blade in food processor. Add cream cheese, sugar, eggs, sour cream, and flour to processor and process until completely smooth and blended. Pour melted chocolate into processor and pulse on and off immediately. Overprocessing will result in a chocolate cheesecake rather than a marble cheesecake.

Pour marbled mixture into cooled pastry shell. Bake in a preheated 350-degree oven for about 1 hour. Turn oven off and allow cheesecake to remain in oven for an additional hour. Refrigerate for at least 6 hours before serving.

Before serving, remove sides from pan. Spread whipped cream over top of cake. Spoon strawberries on top.

**Serves:** 8

# Italian Ricotta Cheese Pie

**PASTRY SHELL**

**2 cups all-purpose flour**
**⅛ teaspoon salt**
**½ cup sugar**
**4 tablespoons butter, cut into 4 pieces**
**3 egg yolks, beaten**
**1 tablespoon milk**
**4 tablespoons water**

**FILLING**

**1½ pounds ricotta cheese**
**1½ cups sugar**
**4 eggs**
**1 teaspoon vanilla extract**
**2 teaspoons lemon juice**
**Grated rind of ½ lemon**
**½ cup semisweet chocolate pieces**
**½ cup glazed citron**

Place metal blade in food processor. Add all ingredients for pastry crust, except milk and water, to processor. Process until the mixture has the consistency of coarse meal. With the machine running, add milk and water, gradually, until mixture forms a ball. Remove dough. Refrigerate dough for 3 to 4 hours.

Place all ingredients for filling, except chocolate and citron, in food processor and, using metal blade, blend until smooth.

Divide dough in half. Roll out half of dough and fit into the bottom of a 9 or 10-inch pie plate, making sure to have a

1-inch overhang of dough around the edge of the pie plate. Fill crust with ricotta mixture and stir in chocolate pieces and citron.

Roll out remainder of dough for a lattice top. To make lattice, cut narrow strips of pastry and weave them, forming the latticework, on floured board or piece of waxed paper. Slip lattice on top of pie. Trim and seal edges by folding bottom crust over top. Flute edges. Bake in a preheated 350-degree oven for 50 to 60 minutes or until top is puffed and golden brown.

**Serves:** 8

# Hungarian Dilly Cheesecake

**CRUST**

**1¼ cups all-purpose flour**
**½ pound butter, cut into 10 to 12 pieces**
**2 egg yolks**
**⅓ cup sugar**
**½ teaspoon baking powder**
**Grated rind of ½ lemon**
**Pinch of salt**
**2 tablespoons sour cream**

**FILLING**

**2 eggs, separated**
**½ pound pot cheese**
**½ cup sugar**
**¼ teaspoon vanilla extract**
**1 tablespoon lemon juice**
**4 tablespoons minced fresh dill**
**1 egg beaten with 1 tablespoon milk**

*To Make Crust:*

Place metal blade in food processor. Add flour and butter to processor and process until mixture has the consistency of coarse crumbs. Add egg yolks, sugar, baking powder, lemon rind, salt, and sour cream. Process until mixture is blended. Remove dough and refrigerate for 30 minutes.

Take chilled dough and roll out three-quarters of it in a 9-inch square baking pan. Prick dough with a fork at the bottom and bake in a preheated 375-degree oven for 10 minutes.

*To Make Filling:*

If your processor has an accessory that beats egg whites, use it to beat egg whites until they are stiff, or beat egg whites until stiff with a hand beater. Reserve beaten egg whites.

Place metal blade in food processor. Add egg yolks, cheese, sugar, vanilla, and lemon juice to food processor and, pulsing on and off, blend thoroughly. Remove to bowl and fold in beaten egg whites. Stir in dill.

*To Assemble Cheesecake:*

Spread cheese filling on partially baked dough. Roll out remainder of the dough for a lattice top. To make lattice, cut narrow strips of pastry and weave them, forming the latticework, on a floured board or piece of waxed paper. Slip lattice on top of cheesecake. Brush latticework strips with egg-milk mixture.

Place cake in a preheated 375-degree oven and bake for an additional half hour. Allow cake to cool, and cut into squares before serving.

**Serves:** 6 to 8

# Espresso Black Bottom Pie

**CRUST**

**18 Zweiback biscuits, broken into large pieces**
**2 tablespoons sugar**
**⅓ cup melted butter**

**FILLING**

**2 tablespoons cornstarch**
**¼ cup sugar**
**¼ teaspoon salt**
**2 cups brewed espresso coffee**
**4 egg yolks**
**2 one-ounce squares semisweet chocolate, melted**
**1 envelope unflavored gelatin**
**1 teaspoon vanilla extract**
**4 egg whites**

**1 cup heavy sweet cream**
**½ cup sugar**
**2 tablespoons sugar**

*To Make Crust:*

Place metal blade in food processor. Add Zweiback pieces to processor and process until you have fine crumbs. Add sugar and continue processing until well mixed. Pour crumb-sugar mixture into a bowl and add butter, mixing until crumbs are moistened. Press mixture firmly into bottom and sides of an ungreased 9 inch pie plate and chill.

*To Make Filling:*

In a 1-quart saucepan, mix cornstarch, sugar, and salt. Stir in coffee and egg yolks. Stir constantly over low heat until sauce bubbles and thickens. Remove from heat; pour 1 cup of the sauce into a small bowl and stir in melted chocolate. In a cup, mix gelatin and ¼ cup water. Stir gelatin mixture into remaining hot coffee sauce. Stir in vanilla. Cool chocolate and coffee mixtures separately.

Spread cool chocolate mixture evenly into bottom of crumb-lined pie plate.

If your processor has an accessory that beats egg whites, use it to beat egg whites until stiff and glossy, or beat egg whites until stiff and glossy with a hand beater. Reserve beaten egg whites. Wash processor bowl and metal blade, dry thoroughly, and place in freezer with heavy cream. (While only some machines can do a proper job on egg whites, most processors now can beat cream so that it's thick enough for this recipe.) Fold beaten egg whites into coffee mixture which will have thickened as it cools. Spread coffee mixture over chocolate mixture in pie plate.

*To Assemble Pie:*

Place metal blade in food processor. Add heavy cream to processor and whip, adding sugar gradually through feed tube until cream is thick. If your machine comes with beater accessory, use instead of metal blade. Garnish pie with whipped cream.

**Serves:** 6 to 8

# Southern Pecan Pie

**1 eight-inch unbaked All-American Piecrust (see page 204)**
**½ cup sugar**
**2 tablespoons butter**
**2 eggs**
**2 tablespoons all-purpose flour**
**¼ teaspoon salt**
**1 teaspoon almond extract**
**1 teaspoon vanilla extract**
**1 cup light corn syrup**
**2 cups pecans**

Prepare pie crust dough, fit into an 8-inch pie plate, and set aside.

Place metal blade in food processor. Add all filling ingredients, except pecans, to processor and blend thoroughly. Add 1½ cups pecans and process briefly, pulsing on and off, until pecans are coarsely chopped.

Pour filling into pie crust and sprinkle remaining pecans on top. Bake in a preheated 350-degree oven for 30 to 45 minutes or until filling is set.

**Serves:** 6

# French Apple Pie

**6 large tart apples, peeled, cored, and cut into quarters**
**¼ cup raisins**
**¾ cup brown sugar**
**1 tablespoon all-purpose flour**
**1 tablespoon lemon juice**
**1 teaspoon cinnamon**
**¼ teaspoon nutmeg**
**2 nine-inch Pâté Brisée Sucrée crusts unbaked (see pages 202–203)**
**1 tablespoon butter**

Place slicing disc in food processor. Slice apples and remove to bowl. Add raisins, brown sugar, flour, lemon juice, cinnamon, and nutmeg to apples and stir thoroughly.

Spoon apple mixture into prepared pie shell. Dot with butter. Cover filling with top crust. Press to seal, and flute edges. Prick top generously with a fork. Bake in a preheated 400-degree oven for 35 minutes or until brown.

**Serves:** 8

# Bill Mayer's Spicy Lettuce Bars with Lemon Frosting

**LETTUCE BARS**

**¼ head iceberg lettuce, cut into pieces**
**1½ cups all-purpose flour**
**2 teaspoons baking powder**
**½ teaspoon baking soda**
**½ teaspoon salt**
**⅛ teaspoon ground cardamom**
**⅛ teaspoon ground ginger**
**1 cup sugar**
**½ cup salad oil**
**1½ teaspoons grated lemon rind**
**2 eggs**
**½ cup walnuts**

**LEMON FROSTING**

**1½ cups confectioner's sugar**
**¼ teaspoon lemon extract**
**½ teaspoon grated lemon rind**
**3 tablespoons milk**
**1 tablespoon sweet butter**

*To Make Lettuce Bars:*

Place metal blade in food processor. Add lettuce to processor and chop. Sift flour with baking powder, baking soda, salt, cardamom, and ginger. Add to processor and combine. Gradually add sugar, oil, and lemon rind to processor and combine. Add eggs one at a time and continue processing. Add walnuts and process mixture until well blended and walnuts are coarsely chopped.

Spoon batter into a greased 9×13-inch pan. Bake in a preheated 350-degree oven for 30 minutes. Cool and cut into bars. You should have 12 to 15 bars.

*To Make Lemon Frosting:*

Place metal blade in food processor. Add all ingredients to processor and blend until mixture is thoroughly smooth. Spread on Lettuce Bars.

# Crêpes Filled with Jam

**1 cup all-purpose flour**
**¼ cup sugar**
**3 eggs**
**2 tablespoons melted butter**
**1½ cups milk**
**⅛ teaspoon salt**
**2 teaspoons grated lemon rind**
**½ pound butter**
**8 ounces of jam**

Place metal blade in food processor. Add flour, sugar, eggs, and butter to processor. Turn machine on and add the milk gradually. Add salt and lemon rind and continue processing until batter has the consistency of light cream. Pour crêpe batter into a bowl or pitcher and let it rest in the refrigerator for 2 hours before using.

*To cook crêpes:*

Lightly butter one or two 6-inch teflon-coated skillets. Using a small ladle, spoon enough batter into pan to coat bottom. Tilt pan so crêpe batter spreads evenly. Cook until lightly browned and then slide out of pan onto a flat plate. Allow crêpe to cool, then fill with your favorite jam (homemade apricot is best; see page 246), and roll.

Place rolled crêpes in a baking dish and heat for 15 minutes in a preheated 350-degree oven before serving. Crêpes may be made the day before, and as you become adept at crêpe making, you'll be able to use two crêpe pans without any trouble.

**Serves:** 8 (2 crêpes apiece)

# An Abundance of Cookies

*When preparing cookie dough in your food processor, be careful not to overprocess. Pulse on and off, blending ingredients together quickly. Overprocessed cookie dough will result in heavy cookies.*

## Anise Cookies

**¾ cup sugar**
**4 tablespoons butter**
**¼ cup sour cream**
**1 egg**
**1 teaspoon vanilla extract**
**1 teaspoon anise extract**
**1¼ cups all-purpose flour**
**½ teaspoon baking soda**
**¼ teaspoon salt**

Place metal blade in food processor. Add sugar and butter to processor and process until light and smooth, about 30 seconds. Add sour cream, egg, vanilla, and anise, and pulse on and off until well blended. Combine flour, baking soda, and salt. Add mixture to processor, pulsing on and off until just blended.

Drop tablespoonfuls of cookie mixture onto a buttered cookie sheet. Bake in a preheated 350-degree oven for 10 to 12 minutes.

**Yield:** Approximately 24 cookies

# Sugar Cookies

**¼ pound butter, cut into 6 or 8 pieces**
**1 cup sugar**
**1 egg**
**1 tablespoon light sweet cream**
**½ teaspoon vanilla extract**
**½ teaspoon salt**
**1 teaspoon baking powder**
**1½ cups all-purpose flour**

Place metal blade in food processor. Add butter and sugar and process until light and smooth, about 30 seconds. Add egg, cream, and vanilla extract, and pulse on and off until well blended. Combine salt, baking powder, and flour. Add mixture to processor, pulsing on and off, until just blended.

Drop tablespoonfuls of cookie mixture onto a buttered cookie sheet. Bake in a preheated 375-degree oven for about 8 minutes.

**Yield:** Approximately 24 cookies

**SUGAR COOKIE VARIATIONS**

*Walnut Cookies:* Add ⅓ cup finely chopped walnuts

*Coconut Cookies:* Add ½ cup finely chopped coconut

*Lemon Cookies:* Add ½ teaspoon lemon extract, plus 2 teaspoons grated lemon rind, and omit vanilla

*Maple Cookies:* Use crushed maple sugar in place of white sugar

*Christmas Cookies:* Sprinkle with colored sugar while cookies are still hot

*Raisin Cookies:* Add ½ cup chopped raisins

# Chocolate Chunk Cookies

*Chocolate chip cookies may be great, but Chocolate Chunk Cookies are even better. If you want them to be really special, use deep, dark, bittersweet chocolate bars from Switzerland.*

**½ cup sugar**
**8 ounces bittersweet chocolate bars**
**1 cup firmly packed brown sugar**
**¼ pound plus 4 tablespoons butter**
**2 eggs**
**2 teaspoons vanilla extract**
**2¼ cups all-purpose flour**
**1 teaspoon baking soda**
**½ teaspoon salt**

Place metal blade in food processor. Add ¼ cup sugar. With machine on, drop chocolate through feed tube into processor. Process only until chocolate is broken into large chunks. Remove sugar and chocolate from processor and reserve.

Place remainder of sugar, brown sugar, and butter in processor. Using metal blade, process until light and smooth, about 30 seconds. Add eggs one at a time to processor, pulsing on and off after each egg is added until mixture is blended. Add vanilla and pulse on and off twice.

Combine flour, baking soda, and salt. Add flour mixture to processor. Pulse on and off until just blended. Do not overprocess, or cookies will be heavy. Spoon cookie batter into a bowl and stir in reserved chocolate-sugar mixture. Dough will be stiff.

Drop batter by heaping tablespoonfuls onto an ungreased cookie sheet, about 2 inches apart. Flatten slightly. Bake in a preheated 350-degree oven for about 12 minutes, or until cookies are delicately brown.

**Yield:** Approximately 24 cookies

# Peanutty Peanut Butter Cookies

**1½ cups shelled peanuts**
**1 cup firmly packed brown sugar**
**½ cup peanut butter**
**¼ pound plus 4 tablespoons butter (1½ sticks)**
**2 eggs**
**¼ cup plain yogurt or milk**
**2½ cups all-purpose flour**
**1½ teaspoons baking powder**
**½ teaspoon salt**

Place metal blade in food processor. Add peanuts. Pulse on and off for 5 seconds or until peanuts are chopped into large pieces. Remove peanuts and reserve. Add brown sugar, peanut butter, and butter to processor. Process until light and smooth, about 30 seconds. Add eggs one at a time, pulsing on and off after each egg is added until well blended. Add yogurt (or milk), pulsing on and off once or twice. Combine flour, baking powder, and salt. Add flour to bowl. Pulse on and off until just blended. Stir in reserved peanuts while scraping down sides of bowl. Dough should be stiff.

Drop batter by heaping tablespoonfuls onto ungreased cookie sheets about 2 inches apart. Flatten slightly. Bake in preheated 350-degree oven for about 15 minutes.

**Yield:** Approximately 24 cookies

# Pot De Crème

*A* pot de crème *that requires no cooking, and can be prepared in a matter of minutes in a food processor! This is an especially delightful dessert when served in tiny* pot de crème *dishes. Try the recipe first, and if you like it, you might consider it worthwhile to invest in the little porcelain pots that will make this dessert taste even better.*

**1 six-ounce package semisweet chocolate pieces**
**½ cup hot brewed coffee**
**4 eggs**
**¼ cup sugar**
**1 teaspoon brandy or rum**
**4 tablespoons heavy cream**
**1 cup whipped cream (optional)**

Place metal blade in food processor. Add chocolate to processor. Turn machine on and pour hot coffee through feed tube. Process 10 seconds. Add eggs, sugar, brandy, and heavy cream to processor. Continue to process for 20 seconds or until thoroughly blended. Spoon into 6 *pot de crème* cups or dessert dishes. Refrigerate 8 hours or overnight. Garnish with whipped cream if desired.

**Serves:** 6

# Peachy Torte

**4 medium peaches (about 1¼ pounds), peeled, sliced, and pitted**
**4 egg yolks**
**1 cup sugar**
**2 teaspoons lemon juice**
**2 tablespoons peach liqueur (optional)**
**1 cup heavy cream**
**2 tablespoons sugar**
**1 teaspoon vanilla**
**9 meringue cookies**
**2 peaches**
**½ cup raspberry jelly, melted**

Place metal blade in food processor. Add peaches to processor. Process about 40 seconds or until pureed. Add egg yolks and sugar to processor and process 10 seconds, or until thoroughly blended. Pour mixture into the top of a double boiler. Cook over simmering water until thickened, stirring constantly. Add lemon juice, and liqueur if desired. Cool in refrigerator for 15 minutes.

While peach mixture is cooling, place clean dry food processor bowl, metal blade, and heavy cream in the freezer. Chill 10 to 15 minutes. Place metal blade in bowl, and pour chilled cream into cold bowl. Add sugar and vanilla. Process until cream thickens, about 30 to 40 seconds. (If your machine comes with beater accessory, use instead of metal blade.)

Fold thickened cream into chilled peach mixture. Pour into 8-inch springform pan. Arrange meringue cookies on top, pressing into mixture slightly. Place in freezer for about 2 hours, or until firm. At serving time, remove from freezer. Slice and arrange remaining peaches on top. Glaze with melted jelly. Cut into wedges, serve at once.

**Yield:** 8 servings

# Raisin Pound Cake

**½ pound butter, cut into pieces**
**2 cups sugar**
**4 eggs**
**3 cups all-purpose flour**
**1½ teaspoon baking powder**
**½ teaspoon baking soda**
**¼ teaspoon salt**
**½ cup milk**
**½ cup sour cream**
**2½ teaspoons vanilla extract**
**1 cup raisins**

Place metal blade in food processor. Add butter and sugar to processor. Process until light and smooth, about 30 seconds. Add eggs one at a time, pulsing on and off after each egg is added, until well blended.

Combine flour, baking powder, baking soda, and salt. Add 1 cup flour mixture to processor. Pulse on and off until just blended. Scrape down sides of bowl. Add milk and 1 cup flour mixture to bowl. Process as above. Do not overprocess.

Add sour cream, vanilla extract, and remaining flour. Pulse on and off once or twice, or just until blended. Stir in raisins while scraping down the sides of bowl with spatula.

Spoon batter into greased and floured 10-inch Bundt or tube pan. Bake in preheated 325-degree oven for 1 hour, or until toothpick inserted in center comes out clean.

**Yield:** 1 ten-inch pound cake

# Frosted Deep Chocolate Cake

**¼ pound plus 4 tablespoons butter, cut into pieces**
**1¾ cup sugar**
**3 eggs**
**1 teaspoon vanilla extract**
**2 one-ounce squares semisweet chocolate, melted**
**2 cups all-purpose flour**
**1 teaspoon baking powder**
**1¼ teaspoon baking soda**
**½ cup cocoa**
**1 cup buttermilk, or sour milk***
**1 cup semisweet morsels**

Place metal blade in food processor. Add butter and sugar. Process until light and smooth, about 30 seconds. Add eggs one at a time, pulsing on and off after each egg is added until well blended. Add vanilla and melted chocolate. Process 10 seconds or until blended.

Combine flour, baking powder, baking soda, and cocoa. Add one-half flour mixture to processor. Pulse on and off until just blended. Scrape down sides of bowl. Add milk and remaining flour to processor, pulsing on and off until just blended. Stir in chocolate morsels while scraping down sides of bowl again.

Spoon mixture into 2 greased and floured 8-inch round cake pans. Bake in preheated 350-degree oven for 30 to 35 minutes, or until toothpick inserted in center comes out clean. Allow cakes to cool and remove from pans. Frost with Chocolate Butter Cream Frosting (see page 281).

**Serves:** 8 to 10

* If you don't have buttermilk, you can make sour milk by adding 1 teaspoon lemon juice or vinegar to 1 cup of milk. Stir. May be used immediately.

# Chocolate Butter Cream Frosting

**1 pound confectioner's sugar**
**¼ pound butter, cut into 4 pieces**
**1 teaspoon vanilla extract**
**⅓ cup unsweetened cocoa**
**3 to 4 tablespoons milk**
**3 tablespoons chocolate syrup**

Place metal blade in food processor. Add all ingredients. Process for about 40 seconds, or until all ingredients are blended and smooth.

**Yield:** 2 cups

# Carrot Cake with Cream Cheese Frosting

**1 pound carrots, cleaned and scraped**
**1 cup walnuts**
**1 eight-ounce can crushed pineapple, drained**
**½ cup shredded coconut**
**1¼ cup vegetable oil**
**4 eggs**
**2 cups sugar**
**2 cups all-purpose flour**
**2 teaspoons baking powder**
**1 teaspoon baking soda**
**½ teaspoon salt**
**1 teaspoon cinnamon**
**½ teaspoon nutmeg**
**½ teaspoon allspice**
**⅛ teaspoon ginger**

Place shredding disc in food processor. Grate carrots. Remove disc from bowl. Place metal blade in food processor. Add walnuts, crushed pineapple, and coconut to carrots. Pulse on and off once. Remove carrot mixture to a large bowl and reserve.

Place metal blade in processor again. Add vegetable oil, eggs, and sugar to processor and process briefly until blended.

Combine flour, baking powder, baking soda, salt, cinnamon, nutmeg, allspice, and ginger. Add flour mixture to oil-egg mixture in processor. Process once or twice until blended. Spoon flour mixture from processor into bowl with carrots. Mix thoroughly, combining all ingredients.

Spoon batter into a well-buttered and floured 13×9×3-inch baking pan. Bake in a preheated 350-degree oven for 55 to 65 minutes, or until toothpick inserted in center comes out clean. Allow cake to cool before removing from pan. If you wish, frost with Cream Cheese Frosting.

**Serves:** 15

# Cream Cheese Frosting

**1 eight-ounce package cream cheese, cut into chunks**
**1 pound confectioner's sugar**
**1 teaspoon vanilla**
**1 tablespoon lemon or orange juice**

Place metal blade in food processor. Add all ingredients and process about 40 seconds, or until all ingredients are blended and smooth.

Cream Cheese Frosting is also delicious atop Pumpkin Pear Bread (see page 209).

**Yield:** 2 cups

# Rocky Road Fudge Brownie Cake

**1 cup walnuts**
**¼ pound plus 4 tablespoons (1½ sticks) butter**
**½ cup unsweetened cocoa**
**1½ cups sugar**
**2 eggs**
**1 teaspoon vanilla extract**
**1½ cups all-purpose flour**
**½ teaspoon salt**
**½ teaspoon baking soda**
**1 six-ounce package semisweet chocolate morsels**
**1 cup miniature marshmallows**

Place metal blade in food processor. Add walnuts, pulsing on and off once or twice. Nuts should be chopped into large pieces. Remove nuts from processor and reserve.

Add butter, cocoa, and sugar to processor and, using metal blade, process until mixture is light and smooth, about 30 seconds. Add eggs one at a time, pulsing on and off after each egg is added, until mixture is well-blended.

Combine flour, salt, and baking soda. Add to cocoa-egg mixture in processor. Pulse on and off until just blended. Do not overprocess.

Add chopped nuts and chocolate morsels, pulsing on and off twice. Scrape down sides of bowl making sure nuts and chocolate morsels are distributed throughout the cake batter.

Spoon mixture into a greased and floured 8-inch square cake pan. Bake in a preheated 350-degree oven for 45 to 55 minutes. Cool for 10 minutes. Remove from pan. Spread marshmallows over brownies, they will melt into brownies. Cut into squares.

**Yield:** Approximately 12 brownies

# Fresh Plum Sauce

*Fresh plum sauce can be the basis of many marvelous desserts. Serve the sauce over a salad of sliced fresh fruits or use it as a dip for thick slices of pound cake. Spooned over vanilla ice cream, it's the perfect end to a summer's day lunch or dinner.*

**2 pounds ripe, red plums, pitted and sliced**
**1 cup firmly packed brown sugar**
**1 tablespoon lime juice**
**1 tablespoon cornstarch**

Heat plums over low heat in a large saucepan until the juices begin to flow, about 1 minute, stirring constantly. Add sugar, raise heat to medium, and allow plums to come to a boil. Reduce heat, cover, and cook for 8 to 10 minutes, or until plums have softened.

Place metal blade in food processor, spoon plums and juice into processor and process until plums are completely pureed. Return plum puree to saucepan. Combine lime juice and cornstarch, blending until smooth. Stir lime-cornstarch mixture into plum puree. Stir well and cook for an additional 3 minutes, or until plum sauce has thickened. Chill before serving.

**Yield:** Approximately 3 cups

# INDEX